God So Enters into Relationships That . . .

D1566691

God So Enters into Relationships That . . .

A Biblical View

Terence E. Fretheim

Fortress Press

Minneapolis

Cover Image: Footprints on the Beach by zulufriend. iStock © 2013.
Cover Design: Alisha Lofgren

Print ISBN: 978-1-5064-4836-7
Ebook ISBN: 978-1-5064-4837-4

CONTENTS

Part I

■■■

God and Relationship

1

What We Mean by "Relationship"

A key word for any significant discussion about the God of the Bible is "relationship." Indeed, the category of relationship is central to Israel's theological reflection regarding God. What did the writers intend by speaking of the biblical God in relational terms? Think of relationships you have with others—the best relationships. Picture one person with whom you are close. What makes that relationship good? What makes it a genuine relationship? What makes it the kind of relationship in and through which God would empower you to live and work? How might you answer such questions if the relationship of which you are speaking is with God? When we use the language of relationship for God, what are its most basic characteristics?

One of my basic questions for this study is this: When we use the language of relationship in speaking of the God of the Old Testament, what do we mean by the word "relationship"? For the Old Testament, relationships constitute life itself; through relationships all things are woven together like a spider web. Interrelatedness is a basic characteristic not only of the relationship between God and people (and between God and the world) but also of the very nature of the created order. To live in a genuinely relational world inevitably means that every creature will be affected by the activity of every other; each creature is caught up in the interconnected life of all.

Interrelatedness is a basic characteristic not only of the relationship between God and people (and between God and the world) but also of the very nature of the created order.

This understanding of relationship places a key question on the table: What does it mean for God to be a faithful member of this relationship with Israel (and the world)? Communities and relationships can be of many kinds, from healthy and good to abusive and poisonous. What are the characteristics of a *genuine* relationship? A genuine relationship is presumably the only kind of relationship that God, being God, can have with the world, and such a relationship is certainly that for which we all (including God) yearn.

Think of the relationship God has established with you. Typically, questions abound about the nature of the God–person relationship. What kind of relationship is that for you? What kind of relationship is it for God? What happens to our understanding of the God of the Bible if we take the word "relationship" seriously? What does it mean for God to make a commitment to you in such a relationship?

On the one hand, God is imaged by many readers as a distant and aloof landLord—indeed often an absentee landLord—sitting on the front porch of heaven, watching the world go by. And you know how it is with absentee landlords: your calls are seldom returned and nothing much gets done.

On the other hand, God is (too often) imaged as being in absolute control of the world, even to the point of micromanagement.[1] It is all too often claimed that whatever God wills for the world and its creatures gets done, come what may. I have encountered such a perspective in many settings, within and outside of the church. Such an understanding of God has often created barriers for people in their theological reflections. As a student once put it to me: If God is in control, then given how unruly we often are and how unruly the world of nature often is, wouldn't we have to score God as a crashing management failure?

Across theological disciplines these days—indeed in every aspect of our churchly speaking—the word "relationship" peppers the conversation. "Our relationship with God" and "our relationship with Jesus Christ" are well-worn phrases. Such relational interests and the common language used in talk about God are also driven by the increased recognition of the connectedness of our life together. One might note the popular and scholarly energies increasingly given to the interdependence of our world, evident in, say, environmental scholarship. This connectedness is also evident in such varied matters as the global impact of natural disasters and interhuman disasters (9/11, for example), the rippling effects of environmental and economic crises, and the use of the internet. And everyone seems to be reading a smartphone wherever they are. Connected, connected, connected!

We are fast moving from "six degrees of separation"— wherein each of us is supposedly no more than six persons removed from knowing anyone else in the world—to, we might say, five degrees of separation. This shift raises a key question: How should that increasingly intense relational reality, experienced by all, shape our language about God and its implications for life? Is the God we confess attractive to the increasingly interdependent audience for whom relational categories are so integral to self-understanding and life? If we were more deliberate and careful in our talk about a God in relationship, God-talk (in the Bible or outside of it) might become more meaningful to people, and their relationship with God might become more serious.

There will always be some disjunction between God and our language for God, not least the language of relationship. In all such reflection, we need to remember that this is a relationship of "unequals"; it is an asymmetrical relationship. God is God and we are not. God outdistances all our language about relationship. But let it also be said that God's transcendence is not compromised by the language of relationship. To use Abraham Heschel's language, "God remains transcendent in his immanence, and related in his transcendence."[2] We should not think that God is transcendent *and* in relationship, but that God is transcendent *in* relationship. God is not less than God in the relationships into which God enters: God is the Holy One *in the midst of* Israel (Isaiah 12:6; Hosea 11:9).[3]

What if we took the word "relationship" seriously? What if we spoke of the God-human relationship as real and genuine, a relationship of integrity (the only kind of relationship God can have)? If we made this theological move, what would be the implications of such an understanding? Our God-talk might need to be cleaned up because genuine relatedness would be integral to our talk about God's interaction with the world. I would think we could all agree that we want to keep our theology and our practice, our theology and our leadership roles coherent. A basic consistency among these realities is important not least because we would not want our theology to undercut our practice. I am concerned about the *practical adequacy* of our usual talk about God as we seek to understand our relationships with God more fully.

If what we say about the connectedness of our world is anywhere near the mark, our understanding of God needs to be looked at more carefully in that light. How well does our imaging of God (within and outside of the church) connect with people who are a part of this interrelated world? Elizabeth Johnson is helpful in considering these issues:

> Religions die . . . when they lose the power to interpret convincingly the full range of present experience in the light of their idea of God. The truth about God is tested by the extent to which the idea of God currently available [in the church] takes account of accessible reality

and integrates the complexity of present experience into itself. If our idea of God does not keep pace with developing reality, the power of experience pulls people on and the god dies, fading from memory.[4]

Johnson raises an issue worth pondering relative to the increased usage of the language of relationship: Is the language of relationship, so integral to life at all levels of experience, a sufficient part of the theological discussion about God these days? And, importantly, what do we mean when we use that language?

The language of interrelatedness is integral not only to the world of creatures; it is also true of God—God's own identity. Whether one takes a basic Old Testament understanding of God in community ("Let *us* make humankind," Genesis 1:26) or a Christian understanding of Trinity, such understandings are integral to developments along a trajectory of reflection about God in community. Both God and the world's creatures are who they are because of relationships of which they are a part. Their very identities are shaped in significant ways by this reality.

> Both God and the world's creatures are who they are because of relationships of which they are a part.

2

What Kind of God?

It is not enough to say you believe in God; what matters, finally, is *the kind of* God in whom you believe. The kind of God about whom you speak will shape your life and your vocation. One way to get inside this conversation is to explore the various metaphors for God in the Bible. I invite you to think of the images for God that you most commonly use in your teaching, preaching, praying, and conversation. I don't think there is much question that the bulk of the metaphors for God in the Bible are highly relational. The language for God is commonly drawn directly from the realm of human life, arising out of the dynamic interplay of human experience and the God who is believed to be active in and through this experience. Generally speaking, these relational metaphors are ordinary, common, everyday, earthly—indeed deeply secular—rather than dramatic, heavenly, religious, or even theological. Think of the language of home and work, family and friends, village and city and nation, the language of personal and interpersonal experience. It is drawn from spheres such as the human personality (thinking, speaking, feeling, willing), personal activity (use of mouth, hand, arm, eyes), and the family (husband-wife, parent-child, both father and mother). We find in Scripture examples of God speaking, using personal images:

> For a long time I have held my peace,
>   I have kept still and restrained myself;
> Now I will cry out like a woman in labor,
>   I will gasp and pant. (Isaiah 42:14)

> As a mother comforts her child, so I will comfort you,
>   you shall be comforted in Jerusalem. (Isaiah 66:13)

These kinds of relational images were believed by readers to be most revealing of a God who has deeply entered into the life of the world and is related to every creature that is not God. We need to use as many relational metaphors for God as possible in order to portray the fullness that is God and to make lively connections with life as it is usually lived.

> We need to use as many relational metaphors for God as possible in order to portray the fullness that is God and to make lively connections with life as it is usually lived.

The sociopolitical spheres of life also need special attention in such a conversation (king, judge, friend). God as "friend" is a particularly striking source for metaphors these days in view of the Facebook culture. Note Jesus's words to his disciples in John 15:15 (echoing Isaiah 41:8; see James 2:23): "I do not call you servants any longer . . . but I have called you friends." What difference might it make in people's understanding of God if we more regularly used the image of friend for God or talked about God in such a way that people could say something like "Yes, God is my friend"? For more than a century and a half, Christians have sung "What a friend we have in Jesus." Unfortunately, all too often people use the word "friend" for Jesus but not for God. It is often forgotten that "Jesus is not an exception in the life of God": Jesus truly reveals who God is![1] And Jesus reveals what God has been about in the life of the world since long before Jesus was born.

While the most pervasive metaphors the Old Testament uses to speak of the God-human relationship are interpersonal, some are drawn from objects that people have made (fortress, shield, lamp, dwelling place, fountain). These metaphors ought not be considered impersonal, for they are often understood as extensions of the persons who brought them into being; hence, they carry a quite personal significance (e.g., Psalms 31:2; 84:11; 90:1; 91:1–6). Metaphors are also drawn from the animal world in comparable personal terms, as in Psalms 91: "He will cover you with his pinions, and under his wings you will find refuge; his faithfulness is a shield and buckler" (v. 4). Even where natural metaphors, such as sun and light, are used for God, they often serve to illumine quite personal matters, such as healing and guiding (e.g., Psalms 27:1; 84:11). Though metaphors such as rock might seem quite impersonal to modern readers, they take on many personal characteristics in the Old Testament, suggesting that Israel saw much greater continuity between the human and nonhuman worlds than we commonly do (but increasingly recognize these days). Even described by such metaphors, God communicates to David (2 Samuel 23:3), hears the psalmist (Psalm 28:1), leads and guides (Psalm 31:3), and has certain personal attributes (Psalm 92:15; Deuteronomy 32:4).

Unfortunately, the Bible is filled with metaphors for God that we have neglected; the book of Psalms alone has over fifty such metaphors. Examine your teaching, praying, and conversation: How many of these metaphors do you hear and use? Personally, I find the metaphors that relate to our vocations in life especially helpful—for example, seamstress (Psalm 139:13), physician (Psalm 41:3), and teacher (Isaiah 30:8). Such metaphors connect very well with people's daily lives. One such metaphor is used in Psalm 96:1: "Sing to the Lord a new song!" Or, to personalize the metaphor: God is a musician. God is one who gives us new songs to sing. Using the Bible as a model, we need to use as many different metaphors for God as we can to help portray the fullness that is God and to make lively connections with life as people actually live it.

When nonhuman creatures are drawn into the use of a metaphor, it is all too often forgotten by readers that the category of relationship remains at the center of such reflection. One thinks of shepherd-sheep ("The Lord is my shepherd," Psalm 23:1) and a mother eagle and her young ("I bore you on eagles' wings and brought you to myself," Exodus 19:4). Even a metaphor such as rock is used in relational terms—God is "the Rock that bore you" (Deuteronomy 32:18).

Because the metaphors we use for God are drawn from life as it is actually lived, they do not have equal staying power. The way we understand these images is strongly influenced by our individual and social circumstances. And so, we should be prepared over time to adjust our use of metaphors in view of changing times and places. For example, take the metaphor of God as king. This can be a useful metaphor in thinking about God, though it is not actually all that common in the Bible. But given the fact that monarchy is outside of much of our contemporary American experience, the value of such a metaphor for our understanding of God has been significantly diminished. Brian Wren, in connection with his hymn-writing, says:

> I don't use divine kingship or Lordship language because that's out of tune with what I believe and out of tune with the world we live in. The use of that language is one of the concerns I have with a lot of so-called praise songs. Divine kingship was once a meaningful political symbol because most governments were monarchies. It made sense to speak of God as king or monarch (it was, of course, always a male monarch). People understood it to mean, for one thing, that since God is king you'd better obey God's earthly representative, the church.[2]

So many of our praise songs pound away at such a royal image of God. But what import does such an image have in a non-monarchial culture such as our own? Perhaps many readers will conclude: God is like the King of Norway or the Queen of

England! Or they will conclude that such images for God are too far removed from actual life to be meaningful or helpful.

I am concerned with the effects such metaphors can have on the understanding of our life and work and interrelationships, not least our relationship with God. Such metaphors will certainly have varying levels of efficacy, for metaphors function differently depending on the hearer. But metaphors will shape our lives, willy-nilly and in ways beyond our knowing, not least because we are asked to walk in God's ways, to be the image of God we in fact are. If we most commonly talk about God as king and/or judge, will not our life and ministry be shaped primarily in those terms? Then hierarchical forms of leadership and relationship are not far away. Think of the effect such images for God have on the lives of people over time. How will people come to view the God of the church and the Bible? Perhaps people will come to see that God is just another adult who is intolerant of my unconventional questions or that God is but another bossy parent ("Wait till your father gets home!").

The use of such metaphors for God also has implications for how we understand human beings. Inasmuch as we are created in the image of a relational God, relationality is a key category for thinking about who *we* are. If we don't use genuinely relational language in our talk about God, that failure may adversely affect how we think about relationships among those who are created in the image of God. We may well have a high view of human relationality, but this talk is all too often subverted and diminished— indeed, maybe even made incoherent—by an understanding of God who is relational only in a perfunctory sense.

Theologian Eberhard Jungel makes an important point: "The more one understands God the more mysterious God becomes. And the deeper one penetrates the mystery the more interesting God becomes."[3] In other words, the more you know about God, the more you know you don't know. It would also follow that the less you know about God, the less of a mystery God is. God is not demystified by further understanding; indeed, the greater the understanding, the more the divine inexhaustibility becomes apparent *and* the more interesting it becomes.

Certainly, God outdistances all of our language about God, and the images and metaphors we use for God always come up short. At the same time, for all that God has revealed to us regarding the divine self, most supremely in Jesus Christ, I think we have only begun to plumb the depths of Scripture regarding the understanding of God it does provide. We can trust Jesus's promise that the Holy Spirit will continue to lead us into all the truth about God (see John 16:13). We certainly have not yet arrived; much biblical work remains to be done and many theological insights are yet to be gained (even "great and hidden things that you have not known," Jeremiah 33:3). May we be given the wisdom to see those insights when they come our way!

> If we don't use genuinely relational language in our talk about God, that failure may adversely affect how we think about relationships among those who are created in the image of God.

15

Relationship and Covenant

Through the lens provided by these various metaphors, the God of the Old Testament is seen to be a highly relational God. Most basically, God is present and active in the world; God enters into a relationship of integrity with that world, especially with Israel; and both world and God are deeply affected by that linkage. In this relationship, God has chosen not to stay aloof, but to get caught up with the creatures in moving toward the divine purposes for creation, and in such a way that God is deeply affected by such an engagement.

Relationship talk is nothing new for Old Testament studies, however. Nearly a century ago, Walter Eichrodt titled the first chapter of his *Theology of the Old Testament* "The Covenant Relationship."[4] But even Eichrodt noted (as have other scholars) that "covenant" cannot be equated with "relationship." It is very clear that the relationship, indeed a faith relationship, between God and Israel (or any individual) *precedes* the establishment of any covenant. For example, Israel is specified as God's people before the covenant at Mount Sinai ("Let my people go," Exodus 7:16; 8:1, 20; 9:1 et al.). The Sinai covenant has to do not with the establishment of a relationship with Israel, but with a formalization of Israel's vocation within an existing relationship.

The Old Testament understands that the God-human relationship is much more basic and much more comprehensive than the word "covenant" allows. "Relationship" is a category that includes "covenant" but is a much more pervasive idea that encompasses many other dimensions of the reality of interrelatedness. This understanding of relationship is also evident in the covenants of God with Noah, Abraham, and David (Genesis 9; Genesis 15; 2 Samuel 7). Each of these covenants is a unilaterally declared divine promise and is *preceded* by divine election, divine deliverance, and the individual's response in faith and worship. These divine promises seem designed to provide a firm grounding, or foundation, upon which existing relationships can more fully develop. In any case, the Old Testament understands the God-human relationship as more comprehensive than the word "covenant" suggests. The idea of relationship is so basic a category in the Bible that it should be placed up front in any overarching consideration of Old Testament theological perspectives involving God and the world's creatures.

> The idea of relationship is so basic a category in the Bible that it should be placed up front in any overarching consideration of Old Testament theological perspectives involving God and the world's creatures.

3

A Relational God

While we often use the word "relationship" for the God-human encounter, we may use it in terms that do not connect very well with our usual understanding regarding personal relationships. All too often, the relationship with God of which we speak does not look very much like our other relationships. The upshot may be that people will experience such a disjunction between their everyday experience of relationship with others and the way in which God is portrayed that the word "relationship," when used of God, becomes meaningless or incoherent.

When we use the language of relationship, again we ask: What does genuine relationship entail? The following claims seem especially pertinent in thinking through these matters from an Old Testament perspective (recalling what it takes for a genuine interhuman relationship, such as a marriage, to thrive). I will weave some practical implications into these considerations, but I emphasize that these points are not fully developed; I hope to say enough to generate reflection and conversation. From one angle of vision, and in view of the discussion to this point, the reader might think of three prominent ways in which the Bible speaks of God and relationship.[1]

1. The God of the Old Testament is a relational being.

God's very identity is relational. From early on in Genesis, the text witnesses that Israel's God is a social being, functioning within a divine community. See the communal references in Genesis 6:4; Isaiah 6:8; Jeremiah 23:18–23; Proverbs 8:22–31. These texts and others witness to the richness and complexity of the divine realm.

The plural language used by God in Genesis 1:26, "Let us make humankind in our image," attests that God is not in heaven alone, and, even more, God is engaged in a relationship of mutuality, often referred to as the "divine council." Human beings are created in the image of a God who chooses to create in such a way that that creative power is shared with those who are not God. In other words, relationship is integral to the identity of God, prior to and independent of God's relationship to the world.

> Human beings are created in the image of a God who chooses to create in such a way that that creative power is shared with those who are not God.

This divine council is also the most natural addressee of God's words in 2:18, "It is not good that the man should be alone." The likely context for this particular divine speaking is that aloneness is not characteristic of God, and hence, the isolated human is not truly in the divine image. Or, in other words, it is not good for the human being to be alone because it would not be good for God either. Only the human being as social and in relationship with other beings is truly correspondent to the sociality of God and what it means to be created in the image of God.

The witness that God is one and unique ("the Lord is our God, the Lord alone," Deuteronomy 6:4; Isaiah 40:18, 25) is not compromised by this recognition of the sociality of God, for God is God, and other members of the divine council are not.[2] Unlike other deities in Israel's environment (cf. Baal), Israel's God is not divided into various divinities or powers. While the language of monotheism may be too theoretical (and dependent upon certain philosophical perspectives), some such formulation is in order. It is historically most consistent to say that these Old Testament perspectives on the social nature of God provided a theological matrix for the development of later theological perspectives, including Trinitarian reflections on these plural references to God.

Developments in Israel's understanding of the oneness of God may certainly be discerned in various texts. Isaiah 40–55 provides the clearest formulations (e.g., Isaiah 43:10–13). Some gathered statements that reveal such an understanding of God include the following: God's relationship with the world is such that the world is full of God. In the words of Jeremiah 23:23–24, "Am I a God near by, says the Lord, and not a God far off? . . . Do I not fill heaven and earth? says the Lord." In other words, more specifically, the world is full of the steadfast love of God (Psalm 33:5) and of the glory of God (Isaiah 6:3). One might even say that the world is conceived as the home of God. Where there is world, there God—who is other than world—is lovingly active, working from *within* that world, not working *on* the world from without. From the perspective of Psalm 139, there is no time or place in the world, from the macrocosmic to the microcosmic, where one is beyond the presence of God.

Such an understanding of divine presence carries with it a conviction that the Old Testament does not ever speak of the absence of God in the life of the world.[3] The language of God's forsaking and abandoning (for example, Jeremiah 12:7–13) is not a move from presence to absence, but a move to distance, to a less intense presence, with the effect that the forces that make for death and destruction will often have their way. The judgment texts in Jeremiah make especially clear that divine distance does not mean absence; in these texts God's forsaking of Israel issues in the form of an especially intense experience of the wrath of God.

2. This relational God freely enters into relationships with (all) the creatures.

God has established a relationship with the creatures (both human and nonhuman), including a special relationship with Israel.

As noted, the various biblical metaphors for God—with few, if any, exceptions—have relatedness at their core. These kinds of relational images for God reveal a God who has entered deeply into the life of the world and is present and active in the common life of individuals and communities. The pervasive use of anthropomorphic/anthropopathic language for God is especially significant in this connection. This kind of language stands together with the more concrete metaphors used for God in saying something important about God. God is a living and dynamic being whose ways of relating to the world are best conveyed in the language of human personality and activity.

The human being, with all of the capacities for relationship, is biblically believed to be the most appropriate image of God in the life of the world. This relational God of the Old Testament is not first and foremost the God of Israel, but the God of the world. God was in relationship with the world before there ever was an Israel, and so God's relationship with Israel must be understood as a subset, albeit a deeply significant one, within this more inclusive and comprehensive divine-world relationship. God's acting and speaking are especially focused in Israel, but this divine activity is a strategic, purposive move for the sake of the entire world

> God is a living and dynamic being whose ways of relating to the world are best conveyed in the language of human personality and activity.

order (see Genesis 12:3, "in you all the families of the earth will be blessed").

The opening chapters of Genesis illustrate this divine perspective: God involves the creatures in creational tasks (Genesis 1–2); God walks in the garden and engages the human (3:8–13); God ameliorates Cain's judgment (4:15); God suffers a broken heart (6:6); God limits the divine options for responding to sin and evil (8:21–22). And readers are not yet encountering Abraham and Israel! Such divine actions and relationships are not unique to Israel. The rest of the book of Genesis witnesses to this relational kind of God. God genuinely interacts with "outsiders," including Hagar (16:7–13), Abimelech (20:3–7), and Pharaoh (41:15–36); God responds to the prayers of the chosen people on behalf of the unchosen (18:22–33; cf. Exodus 32:7–14; Numbers 14:19–20). For both chosen and unchosen, encompassing all human beings and their activity, this divine-human relationship has a genuinely interactive character.

The importance of such relational language is sharply evident in the prohibition of images (see Exodus 20:4–6, "You shall not make for yourself an idol . . ."). The basic concern of this prohibition is to protect God's *relatedness*. In the words of Psalm 135:15–17, the idols "have mouths, but they do not speak; they have eyes, but they do not see; they have ears, but they do not hear" (see also Psalm 115:5–7; Jeremiah 10:4–5). With the idols there is no deed or word, no real presence, no genuine relationship. This relational understanding is consistent with the way the Old Testament speaks of a legitimate concrete image— namely, the human being (Genesis 1:26). The human being, with all of its capacities for relationship, is believed to be the only fully appropriate image of God in the life of the world.

3. This relational God has created a world in which all creatures are interrelated.

Every creature stands in a symbiotic relationship with every other creature. This is to say that the category of relationship is basic to an Old Testament perspective of reality. This may be illustrated by the effect of the moral order upon the cosmic order. Human sin has had an adverse effect upon the entire cosmos. (See the references to the natural order in Hosea 4:1–3, especially v. 3, "Therefore the land mourns and all who live in it languish; together with the wild animals and the birds of the air, even the fish of the sea are perishing.") Proper attention to such themes in the Old Testament through the years would have placed its readers in the vanguard regarding ecological issues long ago.

It is also good to see the strong emphasis in Genesis on the relationship between God and the creation and within creation itself. Relationship is not purely a private matter; it is deeply communal in character as well. "Image of God" language in Genesis 1–11 (1:26–28; 5:1–3; 9:6) testifies to a democratization of the human community. Each element is created for a specific purpose—the moon, the sun, and the stars to rule the day and the night (Genesis 1:16), for example. This purpose is not abstract, but a personal presence attuned to the individual circumstance. One way to think of the divine creativity is to speak of God's bringing into being appropriate relationalities.

We live in an evolving and relational universe in which every creature is related to every other—again, a spider web of a world. A relational God makes space for the world *within the divine life* and embraces that relationship in multiple ways. A relational universe may be said to develop within the relational life of God.

Most basically, the Old Testament urges readers to think of God as being in a genuine relationship with every aspect of the creation and intimately involved with every creature. God's presence and activity in the world must be conceived in relation to the history of the nonhuman world as well as that of the human (see Psalm 36:6, where God is said to "save humans and animals alike"). In fact, the Old Testament thoroughly integrates divine presence and action in these histories. God is deeply engaged in every aspect of the life of the world, including the salvation of both humans and nonhumans. In short, the God-world relationship in the Old Testament takes the language of relationship seriously, meaning many Bible readers will need to rethink traditional portrayals of the God of the Old Testament.

Interrelatedness is basic to this community of God's creatures. Each created entity is in symbiotic relationship with every other and in such a way that any act reverberates out and affects the whole, shaking this web with varying degrees of intensity. Being the gifted creatures that we are, human beings have the capacity to affect the web in ways more intense and pervasive than any other creature, positively and negatively. At the same time, God's relationship with *nonhuman* creatures is not minimal, and this reality needs closer attention in view of the increased awareness of the importance of such creatures in our contemporary world.

That the world's creatures are so interrelated makes more complex our attempts to understand how God relates to these creatures. To speak very generally, God so relates to this interrelated world that every movement in the web affects God as well. In Jeremiah 22:1–5, for example, what human beings do with regard to issues of social justice will affect the future of God as well as the future of the world. God will get caught up in these interconnections and work with them for the sake of all creatures. Negative experience on the part of the various creatures of the world will have a negative impact on the life of God. God delights in creaturely responsiveness, is provoked to anger, and weeps with those who weep. Still, God's interaction with emerging realities will always be shaped by God's saving will, God's steadfast love for all, and the divine faithfulness to relationships that God has established.

> Each created entity is in symbiotic relationship with every other.

Or, in other terms, God honors this interrelatedness, and in acting, God takes into account both the order and the play of the creation. Indeed, such is the nature of the divine commitment to the world that God's relationship with Israel (and, in a somewhat different way, with the world) now constitutes the divine identity. The life of God will forever—*forever!*—include the life of the people of God and the life of the world. Since the beginning of creation, God belongs to a community that includes creatures. And in relating to this creaturely community, life for God becomes increasingly complex and interrelated.

Such an understanding of interrelatedness stands over against any notion of a static or mechanistic world. Given the genuineness of these relationships, a degree of open-endedness exists in the created order, which makes room for novelty and surprise, irregularities and randomness. "Time and chance happen to them all" (Ecclesiastes 9:11). To be sure, there are the great rhythms of the world in the witness of Genesis 8:22 (see Jeremiah 31:35–37): seedtime and harvest, cold and heat, summer and winter; day and night. But this natural order includes "play" in the creaturely system; one might speak of a complex, loose causal weave. Job 38–41 constitutes God's own imaging of the complexities of creation; everything does not fit into a neat little schoolroom of nature. Recent learnings from the scientific community demonstrate the rightness of this vision of Job, revealing a cosmos of great complexity, remarkable openness, and a genuine interplay of law and chance.

Models of God's Relationality

In thinking through these relational issues, efforts have been made by readers to speak of three models of the relationship of God to the world.

1. The most common model might be called the double-world image. God has God's own world, which is other than this world. Given that picture, the theological task becomes that of constructing various bridges or channels

in order to bring God's world and our world together. And so, for example, we sing songs such as "He's got the whole world in his hands." In such a relational imaging of God and world, God is outside the world, and like some Charles Atlas or Green Giant, God holds up the world as if it were a baseball. In this image, God is normally not around, but now and again, for reasons that are never very clear, God enters into our world with a "goodie" or a "baddie." This understanding of God's occasional presence keeps one ever looking over one's shoulder and left wondering when God will next "pop into this world."

2. Another common image might be called the Christmas image. Normally, God is off in God's own world, but then, to echo a frequently used image, in Jesus of Nazareth God entered into our time and history and made it the divine home. In this image, God's world only touches our world. All of the world's experience of God somehow has to be channeled through Jesus. But the Old Testament bears witness in many ways, without diminishing the centrality and finality of the Christ event, that it is not the point at which God entered time and history. The world experienced the presence of God pre-Jesus.

3. The Old Testament most sharply witnesses to what might be called a single-world image. God is at home in this world, not in some special God-world. To use the language of Jeremiah 23:23–24, God "fills" heaven and earth. In the words of Isaiah 6:3, "the whole earth is full of his glory." Even more particularly, Psalm 33:5 speaks

of the earth as "full of the steadfast love of the Lord." Such texts make it clear that God is not just here or there; God is always lovingly here and there. All around the world, since time began, God has been present and lovingly at work in the life of every creature.

To use the language of Isaiah 66:1, heaven is God's throne and earth is God's footstool. The heavens and the earth together are God's home and God's environment. Any movement of God from heaven to earth is not a movement from outside the world to inside, but from one part of the world to another; God, who is other than this world (that is, transcendent), always works from within the world and not on the world from without. God is never absent from any aspect of our lives, but is present on every occasion in our lives, and active in every event.

To return to Jeremiah 22:1–5, this text speaks of two possible futures for Israel. The people of God, and indeed the larger creation, through the powers they have been given by God, are capable of shaping the future, indeed the very future of God, in various ways. (Note the two possible futures for God in Jeremiah 22:4–6: "For if you will indeed obey this word . . ."; "But if you will not heed these words . . ."[4]) The future is not simply in God's hands, though that is ultimately the case. God so enters into relationships that God is genuinely affected by what happens to the relationship. For example, the flood is introduced by a grieving God (Genesis 6:6–7, where God "was sorry . . . and it grieved him to his heart"), and later, in prophetic texts, God laments over what has happened to both people (Jeremiah

9:17–18) and environment (e.g., Jeremiah 9:10; 12:7–13). God's response to this creaturely reality is striking indeed: "Let them quickly raise a dirge over us, so that our eyes may run down with tears, and our eyelids flow with water" (Jeremiah 9:18).

Interrelatedness is true not only of the world of creatures; it is also true of God. Through the lens provided by the various images used, the God of the Old Testament is seen to be a highly relational God. Most basically, such an understanding means that God is present and active in the world; that God enters into a relationship of integrity with the world and its creatures, especially with Israel; and that both world and God are affected by that linkage. In this relationship, God has chosen not to stay aloof from the world, but to get caught up with the creatures in moving toward the divine purposes for all of creation.

In sum, God has taken the initiative and freely entered into relationship, both with creation and in covenant with Israel. Having done so, God—who is other than the world—has decisively and irrevocably committed the divine self to be in *a faithful relationship* with that world. Because of who God is, God will certainly honor commitments made to the world and will not suspend these commitments. A promise that God has made is a promise kept—forever.

> God has chosen to get caught up with the creatures in moving toward the divine purposes for all of creation.

God is relational within the very divine life (from a perspective that includes the entire canon, and so, finally, in Trinitarian terms).

And because God has established a relationship with the creatures, the world of creatures that God has created is interrelated.
God is bound to these relationships in ways beyond our knowing.

Given the importance of relational language for thinking
about God and world, we would be advised to think more closely
about the details of this reality. I suggest that the following ten
characteristics are important for thinking through the nature of
the God-world relationship. I list them out at this point and will
develop reflections on each of them along the way. God so enters
into relationships that . . .

- God will be absolutely faithful to the commitments God
  has made.
- God is concerned about our entire selves.
- God will be present with God's creatures at all times and
  in all places.
- God is genuinely affected by what happens to the
  relationship.
- The human will can stand over against the will of God.
- God will be active in the life of the world.
- God recognizes the need for a healthy "space."
- God is not the only one who has something important
  to say.
- God is not the only one who has something important to
  do and the power with which to do it.
- The future is not all mapped out.

I now pursue each of these matters in turn.

Part II

■ ■ ■

God So Enters into Relationships That . . .

4

An Everlasting Faithfulness

God so enters into relationships that God will be absolutely faithful to the commitments God has made.

God will keep promises that he has made to his people. For example, God makes promises to the chosen people in Egypt. The people of God can be certain that God will keep those promises: "I will free you from the burdens of the Egyptians and deliver you from slavery to them. . . . I will bring you into the land that I swore to give to Abraham, Isaac, and Jacob; I will give it to you for a possession" (Exodus 6:6–8). God makes life-changing promises to the people of God, and they can count on God to keep promises.

These divine promises undergird Israel's time in Egypt and are kept during Israel's journey through the wilderness. Life for the people in the wilderness is grounded in a promise God has made. There are better days ahead, the people of God are assured; they can look forward to a life in a land of milk and honey.

Still, living with promises from God does not mean that the chosen people will necessarily *live into* what has been promised. God's promises can be successfully challenged by the people and by what happens in the world. And this reality turns out to be the case for Israel; except for a small minority, the people wandering in the wilderness never live to see the fulfillment of the promise. That some promises seem not to be fulfilled is a characteristic of living in the wilderness. God's word with respect to promises made can be resisted successfully by those who stand in opposition to the work and word of God in the world. God so enters into relationships that God's will does not always get done in the world. Even so, through all of life's journeys, the promises of God remain available for believers to cling to; those who have received the promises can be assured that God is always working toward the fulfillment of promises made.

> God so enters into relationships that God's will does not always get done in the world.

Sometimes we entertain, perhaps even defend, the notion that God is absolutely free and could do anything at any time in any place for any reason—for example, over the course of a wilderness journey or in the midst of a tragedy or disaster. But to think of divine freedom in this "anything is possible for God" way is, actually, to cast doubt on God's promises. Walter Brueggemann claims that "the completed tradition of Jeremiah makes in turn two quite different theological emphases which are impossible to coalesce"—namely, judgment and promise. He makes statements such as "God has withdrawn fidelity" and God "has ceased to care," and points to a "complete absence of fidelity on God's part."[1]

Such challenges provoke important questions. If God is free to break God's promises, does that mean God is no more faithful to relationships than human beings are? What do we teach people about divine faithfulness if we so stress God's freedom that God can "trump" God's own promises? To speak of God's promises, as the biblical texts often do (e.g., God's promises to Noah, Abraham, David; see also Jeremiah 31:35–37; 33:14–26; cf. 14:21), is to speak of a God who places a decisive self-limitation on any talk about divine freedom. God will do what God promises God will do. God will be absolutely faithful to God's own promises.

As we will see, it is precisely because of such divine commitments to promises made that God often grieves over what has happened to the divine relationship with this people. The prophets' testimony to the immense agony and suffering that God experiences in, for example, the exercise of judgment is a demonstration that God is not ever truly free of God's relationship with Israel. Yet, just judgment is not inconsistent with love. Even in the worst of times, God is caught up in this relationship and, therefore, will be positively or negatively affected by how this relationship "goes." God has so entered into the relationship with God's people that God cannot (and will not) cease to be affected by what happens in the divine story with these people. God is "stuck" with what happens to the relationship in view of these commitments.

If God had "radical freedom," as is often claimed, and could do whatever God wanted to do, as has been suggested, then God would not agonize so, either over the breakdown in the relationship or over God's own decisions regarding judgment. If God were truly free of God's own promises, then God would just get up and leave the relationship, for God would be absolutely free to do anything God wanted to do. But according to God's own word to Israel, God is *not* free from the promises given to this people. In the words of Jeremiah 31:3, God loves them with "an everlasting love" (no temporal or other limitations regarding the divine commitments), and God, even in the midst of the worst of judgments that the people of God may experience, has "continued [God's] faithfulness."

> God often grieves over what has happened to the divine relationship with this people.

Because speaking of the freedom of God in such a qualified way, with such limitations, has ethical implications, I suspect the people of God will often attempt to bring such a claim into question. For if God is radically free with respect to relational commitments that God has made, then we who are God's followers should seek to be comparably free! In that case, we can sit loose to our commitments and get on with our unfettered lives. We *will* act in the image of God (as we imagine God)!

To speak accurately of Israel's God is to speak of a God who is absolutely committed to promises made. Indeed, to speak of God's election of Israel and God's promise to be their faithful

God forever places a decisive limitation on any talk about divine freedom. God has exercised freedom in making such promises to Israel in the first place, but having freely made those promises, thereafter God's freedom is truly limited by those promises. On what grounds can such a claim be made about God's promises? God will do what God says God will do; God will be faithful to God's own promises. (At the same time, as noted, God's will in and for the world is not irresistible, so people can act in negative ways in view of which God's promises cannot be kept.) Even more, God's history with Israel through the years has been of such a nature that these people have been caught up into the divine life and have shaped the divine identity. God will *forever* be known as the God of Israel, and this God will be faithful to promises made to God's people.

The extent to which negative developments in the relationship affect not only the (chosen) people, but also animals and vegetation is striking. I return to the language of Jeremiah 9:10–11 (ESV, similiarly NIV; see also Jeremiah 8:19c in context and Jeremiah 9:17–19 with 9:22):

> I will take up weeping and wailing for the mountains, and
> a lamentation for the pastures of the wilderness, because
> they are laid waste so that no one passes through, and
> the lowing of cattle is not heard; both the birds of the air
> and the beasts have fled and are gone.

(These references to nonhuman creatures make for an interesting connection to Israel's wilderness wandering, reflecting God's relationship with such nonhuman creatures.)

God holds tears and anger/judgment together, as people who have suffered the brokenness of intimate relationships commonly do. God mediates judgment in life so sin and evil do not go unchecked in the world, but God does so at great cost to the divine life. God exercises judgment not joyously or with satisfaction, but reluctantly and with great anguish. That divine anger and divine tears go together so often in these texts has considerable theological import. Without the intermittent references to divine tears, God would seem much more distant and removed. Anger accompanied by weeping, while still anger, is different—in motivation and in the understanding of the relationship at stake. God's harsh words of judgment are not matched by an inner harshness. The circumstantial will of God expressed in judgment is always in the service of the ultimate and positive will of God to deliver.

It has been claimed that the time of Israel's wandering in the wilderness is a time of "endangered promises" (as if God can do whatever God wants relative to commitments that God has made). Again and again, the people trust the seeming securities of the past and present more than God's promised future.

> God will remain faithful.

Hence, they experience disasters of various kinds, including plagues, abortive conquests, and snake infestation, that threaten progress toward the goal. But God will remain faithful. The promises of this God are a key theme for living in the wilderness or in the midst of any life journey.

5

Full-Bodied Salvation

God so enters into relationships that God is concerned about our entire selves.

The salvific concern of God is for the salvation of our whole selves and the world of which we are a part; this divine conviction is true both in the present life and in the life to come. Unfortunately, the biblical understanding of "salvation" has often been narrowly conceived by religious people in spiritual terms. In the life of the church, salvation has probably been most associated with the forgiveness of sin. At times, salvation is limited to just that, unfortunately neglecting a great deal of biblical material regarding the all-encompassing nature of salvation. In such a restricted understanding, God's most fundamental activity in the world would have to do with sin and guilt; only secondarily would God be concerned about, say, suffering. But the Bible claims that God's saving work in the world has to do with not only deliverance from one's own sin, but also deliverance from sin's *effects*, both the effects of one's own sin and the effects of the sins of others. And the language of suffering soon fills the room.

Salvation in the Old Testament is always salvation in a full-bodied sense (the New Testament continues this understanding). And so, to not extend that saving activity of God to those who were poor and oppressed was to violate Israel's own history. Helping the poor is a saving act. Such activity is a means whereby God's work of salvation is extended to the larger community. Helping the less fortunate can never be simply a social or political activity; it is also a religious activity in which God has chosen to become involved. Justice is not an end in itself. The exercise of justice stands in the service of salvation for everyone in the community.

> Salvation in the Old Testament is always salvation in a full-bodied sense.

The basis for treating others justly is found in the oft-repeated phrase in the Pentateuch "Remember that you were slaves in the land of Egypt." Think of the two major pillars around which Old Testament texts are gathered: the exodus from Egypt and the exile to Babylon. In the first case, Israel's suffering occurs because of the sins of others, the Egyptians; in the second case, Israel's suffering occurs because of their own sins. Exodus 15:2 uses the language of salvation to speak of what God does on behalf of Israel in delivering them from the Egyptians. Salvation here does not simply have to do with the "spiritual" dimension of life; salvation has to do with any divine action that brings wholeness, life, and well-being, including deliverance from socioeconomic oppressions such as slavery in Egypt.

If we want to draw parallels between Israel's enslaved situation in Egypt and our own dilemmas, it would be important that we not simply focus on our own sin as a problem from which God delivers us. That is another way to be self-serving. Rather, we would do well to ask, What is God's salvation in texts like Exodus 1–15? God's salvation at this point in Israel's life is not forgiveness of sin, but deliverance from an oppressive situation. God did not tell Moses to go to the people of God in Egypt and tell them that their sins were forgiven and that they should get used to the abuse. God said, "Get them out of there!"

This broad understanding of salvation is sharply evident in, for example, the book of Psalms, especially the lament psalms, which comprise over one-third of the Psalter (e.g., Psalms 4–7). These psalms largely have to do with salvation from the sins of others and their ill effects. The prophets understood that the future of Israel's society was deeply dependent upon how the people, both individually and corporately, cared for the less fortunate among them. Israel finally got to the point where the lack of such a concern was among the major factors that led to the destruction of their country and culture. And God the Creator was believed by Israel to be behind this kind of judgment.

It may be tempting to wash our hands of the social and political spheres, to simply disengage. That we so often have difficulty being self-critical about our social and political perspectives may also tempt us to leave these texts that call for justice for the poor alone. On the other hand, we can too easily speak our mind without knowing whereof we speak, avoiding a deep analysis of the situations that need to be addressed. Then again, we can sometimes do nothing more than study and never get anything done. We certainly should devote our energies to discerning the problems we face, and reach out to the needy even if we cannot always agree on local or global strategies. At the least, we should hear and ponder these texts, especially from the prophets. If we do so, few of us will go unchallenged by the deep connections between faith and life that they insist upon. One might generalize to say that where social and political life has an impact on the life, health, and well-being of individuals and communities, there the critical prophetic word needs to be heard.

To draw in the New Testament, this broader understanding of salvation is revealed in the way in which Jesus went about his work. Jesus showed over the course of his ministry that we must think of God's salvation in much more comprehensive terms than we usually do. He used salvation language for the effects of his ministry of healing, not just for the forgiveness of sin. Upon healing people from diseases, for example, Jesus uses salvation language to state what has happened: "Your faith has saved you; go in peace" (Luke 7:50; see also 17:19; 18:42). He reached out and brought salvation in other amazingly diverse ways: deliverance from demon possession, deliverance from storms, economic deliverance from the cheaters who robbed people right within the precincts of the temple. We too often make God's salvation such a small concept, but we should remember that salvation is full-bodied. Jesus Christ lived and died not just to save us from our sins, but to save everything that is related to who we are. Likewise, when we extend the blessings we have received to persons who are less fortunate than we are, we are in some fundamental sense extending God's salvation to them.

Mark Powell helpfully puts the issue like this: "Luke makes no distinction between what we might describe as physical, spiritual or social aspects of salvation. . . . God is concerned with all aspects of human life and relationships, and so salvation may involve the putting right of any aspect of life that is not as it should be."[1] There are dangers here, of course; one could collapse salvation into a political theology or neglect its spiritual dimensions, but just as common among us is a collapsing of salvation into simply a spiritual experience. Jesus in his prophetic ministry helps give shape to our prophetic ministry, and one of the ways to think about this reality is to connect one's ministry/service with the yearnings of those among whom we live—to be free, to be safe, to have a home that one can call one's own, not to have to beg for life's basic needs or human dignity, to be healthy and whole, to be the person God created one to be. This is a more comprehensive understanding of biblical salvation than is typical.

> Jesus Christ lived and died not just to save us from our sins, but to save everything that is related to who we are.

And what about our churchly preaching and teaching? If we suggest that the forgiveness of sin is really the only reality that God is finally concerned about, then do not other dimensions of our talk about God's work among us take on a second-class character? As preachers and teachers, we might give the distinct impression, for example, that God is concerned only about taking care of our sins, and not really concerned about the negative effects of life, such as bodily suffering. But if the work of God in the Old Testament and in Jesus's ministry is any guide, we ought to have a comparable concern about the effects of our own sin and the sins of others, and about all the suffering that that experience can bring our way. As we have noted, Jesus Christ lived and died not only for human sin, but also for human hurt.[2] Jesus Christ lived and died for everything that is you! Salvation in the new heaven and the new earth will be a full-bodied salvation.

6

God's Promise of Presence

God so enters into relationship that God will be present
with God's creatures at all times and in all places.

Another way to think about God's faithfulness in relationship is to speak about God's *promise of presence*. See the
language of Joshua 1:9: "Be strong and courageous; do not be
frightened or dismayed, for the Lord your God is with you
wherever you go." With *you*. *Wherever!* The biblical God is
confessed to be pervasively present, even in the worst of times
and situations.

Yet, this conviction does not mean that God is fully present at every time and place. Cannot the intensity of God's presence vary in different times and places? Is it not possible for
God to be more intensely present at certain times and in some
places and less so at other times and places? If this is the case, are

these differences due only to God's decision to vary the divine intensity of presence? Or is it not possible that God's presence will be negatively or positively affected by who the creatures are and what they do and say? The latter perspective seems most likely to be the case. The biblical conviction is that God chooses to enter into relationships with creatures (and not just human beings) and to be genuinely affected by those relationships in both positive and negative ways. What the creatures do and say can have differing effects on what God can do and say. God can be affected by who the creatures are and what they do and say. God has, from the beginning, entered into this kind of interactive relationship with human beings and other creatures.

We may use language in our speaking and teaching that undercuts this witness regarding divine presence. One all-too-common example is the language of God "intervening" in the world and in the life of Jesus and his disciples. An inference commonly drawn from such interventionist talk is that God is not constantly and pervasively present, but that God intervenes now and again with a "goodie" or a "baddie." At least that's how such an understanding is often heard. And so, when someone is not healed from a disease or saved from disaster or tragedy, those involved may conclude that God made a specific decision not to intervene to help. Accompanying this understanding may be a loss of a sense of God's presence in all times of trouble, suffering, and death. A common result of such thinking is that many people think of God's presence only occasionally. At least that's how the language—that God sometimes intervenes, which logically means that God often chooses not to be present or decides not to intervene—is often heard, even by faithful religious individuals and communities.

When someone is not healed in the wake of our prayers, those involved may conclude that God specifically decided not to intervene to help. But such an understanding fails to recall a pervasive biblical commitment regarding divine presence. As Psalm 139:7–10 makes clear, God is always with us:

Where can I go from your spirit?
Or where can I flee from your presence?
If I ascend to heaven, you are there;
if I make my bed in Sheol, you are there.
If I take the wings of the morning
and settle at the farthest limits of the sea,
even there your hand shall lead me,
and your right hand shall hold me fast.

Such a text means that God is present at every event and active in every occasion; God is present in the big events and also in all the little things that make up our days. God is present in the spiritual moments as well as in the physical and bodily. God is present at our joyous celebrations and also on planes filled with people headed into buildings. Indeed, God is present in the most violent, the most Hitlerian of situations. That claim is a grand witness to the ongoing and pervasive, but not controlling, presence of God. With testimonies

> God is present in the big events and also in all the little things that make up our days.

about God's presence as ubiquitous as these, the followers of this God should be alert not to undercut such a perspective.

Still, such a perspective can also occasion questions about God. Judges 6:12–13, for example, conveys Gideon's puzzlement: "The angel of the Lord appeared to [Gideon] and said to him, 'The Lord is with you, you mighty warrior.' Gideon answered him, 'But sir, if the Lord is with us, why then has all this happened to us?'" Many people, even faithful Christian people, commonly raise such questions—especially in times of suffering and death—in the wake of devastating events. To this issue we will return.

7

Change and Suffering

God so enters into relationships that God is genuinely
affected by what happens to the relationship.

Sometimes the idea is entertained by Bible readers that God
is absolutely free and could do anything at any time in any
place for any reason. But as has been noted, to think of divine
freedom in this way is to cast doubt on God's promises. Is God
free to break God's promises? If so, is God then no more faithful
to relationships than human beings are? What do we teach people about God and the biblical witness if we so emphasize God's
freedom that it "trumps" God's promises? To speak of God's
promises (e.g., to Noah, Abraham, David) is, as we have seen,
to speak of a God who places a decisive limitation on divine
freedom and to attest that God will be faithful to God's own
promises to individuals and communities—come what may!

Throughout the biblical text God is provoked to anger (over five hundred times in the Old Testament and over one hundred times in the New Testament). God laments over the suffering of people and the negative effects on the environment (e.g., Jeremiah 8:22–9:10). God is delighted over positive developments in the world. God is affected by prayers prayed and words spoken. What would God's love mean if God would or could never be affected by what happens to the relationship?

The prophets' testimony to the immense agony and suffering of God in the exercise of judgment is one specific demonstration that God is not truly free of God's relationship with Israel (e.g., Jeremiah 9:10[1]). God is not free of these people, per God's own decision to be faithful. As we noted above, in the perspective of Jeremiah 31:3, God loves God's people with "an everlasting love" and God, even in the midst of the worst of judgments, has "continued [God's] faithfulness."

At least two things need to be said at this point about what it means for God to be in relationship. God is both constant and changing. Is this reality also not commonly true of all interhuman relationships? They are constant in terms of promises made and changing as the relationship develops over time. As we have noted, God will be consistently faithful to promises that God has made. God will always will the best for us, and God's love will be there for us through thick and thin. At the same time, in order to remain true to these commitments, indeed

God is both constant and changing.

to remain true to God's own character, God must change in view of new times and places in and through which God's people move. God must change in order to remain true to who God is.

Many texts witness to such a divine change of mind. For example, God responds to Moses's prayers in the wake of the golden calf debacle by changing the divine mind regarding judgment (Exodus 32:14). This text does not mean that God was convinced by Mosaic logic or that God had not thought of this option before. Rather, God so honors the relationship with Moses, so values it, that God takes a different path into the future. Moses's prayer creates a new situation for God; God has some new ingredients with which to work. God takes the response of the other in the relationship with genuine seriousness.

A more complex example of divine change may be noted in passing: God changes the content of laws between Exodus and Deuteronomy (e.g., see the changes regarding slavery in Exodus 21 and Deuteronomy 15). That is, God revises some of God's own laws in view of new times and places. God is affected by what people say and do and by what happens to them, and God can adjust ways and means (though not ultimate salvific goals) in view of what happens in the relationship.

God and Suffering

That God changes raises the issue of the "affectability" of God, attesting to the kind of relationship God has with the creation. Remarkably often, we think of the suffering of human beings as God's will, sometimes suggesting that God has "sent suffering"

53

for purposes of discipline or some other reason. But Old Testament texts abound regarding God's being affected by the divine experience of the world with the result that at times, God suffers. For God to "'know' the people's sufferings testifies to God's *experience* of this suffering, indeed God's *intimate* experience. . . . For God to *know* suffering is, to follow the metaphorical grain, to allow suffering to enter deeply into the divine being."[2]

It is not often thought by Bible readers that God and suffering were closely linked in pre-Christian literature; hence, the notion of a crucified Messiah is commonly thought to be a distinctively Christian formulation. At the same time, the Old Testament witness to a suffering God seems not to have been taken into sufficient account in this discussion. God did not suffer for the first time in the Christ event; even more, God did not suffer for the sins of the world for the first time on the cross. See Isaiah 43:24–25, for example:

> But you have burdened me with your sins;
>> you have wearied me with your iniquities.
> I, I am He who blots out your transgressions for my own
>> sake,
>> and I will not remember your sins.

The New Testament witness to the finality and universality of Jesus's suffering and death is certainly an advance when compared to Old Testament understandings of God. But it is an advance on an existing trajectory of reflection about a God who suffers. The Christ who suffers and dies on the cross for the sins of the many bears a strong "family resemblance" to the God revealed in the Old Testament, particularly in the prophets. To see the face of God in a crucified man would not have been a radical move for those steeped in Old Testament understandings of God. The kind of God whom the early Christians knew from their scriptures was a God who could know the experience of crucifixion and suffering.

> In opening the divine self up to the vulnerabilities of a close relationship, God experiences suffering.

The Old Testament witness to a suffering God is rich and pervasive. This understanding of God is grounded in a God who has entered deeply into relationship with the world, and with Israel in particular. In opening the divine self up to the vulnerabilities of a close relationship, God experiences suffering because of what happens to that relationship.

Three dimensions of divine suffering may be developed at this point.[3]

1. God suffers *because* the people have rejected God. In such cases, God speaks in traditional lament language (e.g., Isaiah 1:2–3; Jeremiah 2:5, 29–31; 3:19–20; 8:4–7; 9:7–9). Jesus's words over Jerusalem stand in this divine lament tradition: "Jerusalem, Jerusalem, the city that kills the prophets and stones those who are sent to it! How often have I desired to gather your children together as

a hen gathers her brood under her wings, and you were not willing!" (Matthew 23:37).

2. God suffers *with* those who are experiencing suffering. For example, Exodus 3:7: "Then the Lord said, 'I have observed the misery of my people who are in Egypt; I have heard their cry on account of their taskmasters. Indeed, I know their sufferings.'" Also, Jeremiah 31:20: "Is Ephraim my dear son? Is he the child I delight in? As often as I speak against him, I still remember him. Therefore, I am deeply moved for him; I will surely have mercy on him, says the Lord." This is language to which the Immanuel theme might be related.[4]

3. Several texts witness to a divine suffering *for*; see, for example, Isaiah 42:14: "For a long time I have held my peace, I have kept still and restrained myself; now I will cry out like a woman in labor, I will gasp and pant" (see also Hosea 11:7–9). Consider also the previously mentioned Isaiah 43:24–25. God here testifies to being "burdened" with the sins of the people (the verb is *'abad*, to which *'ebed*, "servant," is related). This divine "carrying" of the sins of the people issues immediately in the unilateral announcement of forgiveness "for my own sake." To this text should be linked the "bearing sin" passages of Isaiah 53:4, 11–12 (cf. 1 Peter 2:24). The servant of God thus assumes the role that God has just played.

Many of these divine suffering texts make clear that human sin is not without cost for God. For God to continue to bear the brunt of Israel's rejection, rather than deal with it on strictly legal terms, means continued life for the people. What does such suffering mean for God? In some sense it means the expending of the divine life for the sake of the relationship with the people and their future life together. In the especially striking Isaiah 42:14 ("I [God!] will cry out like a woman in labor, I will gasp and pant"), God acts on behalf of a barren people who are unable to bring their own future into being. God engages in such a giving of self that only one of the sharpest pains known to humankind can adequately portray what is involved for God in bringing to birth the new creation of Israel beyond exile. For this kind of God, the cross is no stranger.

Three factors may be cited relative to the reality of suffering in life and God's having created a dangerous world. Suffering is integral to God's good creation (and has no necessary relationship to sin; as noted in chapter 5, even if there had been no sin in the world, there would be suffering).

1. Human beings are finite creatures, created with limits of intelligence, agility, and strength. When creatures stretch those limits (in, say, education or sports), they may suffer for the sake of gain. As is often said: no pain, no gain.

2. God created a world in which creaturely actions, whether purposeful or accidental, human or nonhuman, may have negative effects on creatures. God can judge the world in and through the created moral order. God's world works in this way.

3. Accidents happen in God's good creation, and creatures can be hurt, and even die, as a result of an experience of that reality. God has not created a risk-free world.

God has created a dynamic world. Think of natural evil (earthquakes, volcanoes, glaciers, storms, bacteria, viruses). Such occurrences and their negative effects are not due to sin, but are present simply because of the way the world God created works. God created a world that can be violent quite apart from human behavior. God created the world good, not perfect. We can still talk about salvation. Most students of this topic would grant that God's good creation was "from the beginning" characterized by "wildness, randomness, risks such as water and the law of gravity. . . . Such natural events as earthquakes, volcanoes, floods, destructive weather patterns, cell mutations, and even potentially deadly viruses were an integral part of the creation before human beings showed up."[5] Such realities have always been a part of God's world, even before sin entered the world's picture. The entrance of sin into the world order merely intensified an already existing dangerous reality.

> **God created the world good, not perfect.**

8

God's Will and Ours

God so enters into relationships that the human will can
stand over against the will of God.

The wilderness, through which Israel journeyed for many
years, was remarkably a place for the revealing of the will
of God. The law is perhaps the most prominent of such revela-
tions during this stretch of Israel's life. Law should be viewed
most fundamentally as a gracious gift of God that gives shape to
Israel's vocation in the world and to the life of all creatures.

I build here on earlier reflections regarding the law as both
constant and changing. In view of changing times and places,
God revises the law—indeed, it could be said that God revises
God!—for the sake of the life and health of an ever-changing
community. God gives the law to the people of Israel to ensure a
life of stability and well-being for all, especially for those who are

disadvantaged. As such, the law is not understood as static; the law moves with the ever-new experiences of the people of Israel as they make their way through life. Even more, the laws change as they encounter the lives of different peoples in different times and places.

We focus initially on biblical law. First, the law God gives to the people of Israel at Mount Sinai is not something new for them. Law has been a part of the life of people from creation onward, beginning with the command "Be fruitful and multiply, and fill the earth and subdue it" (Genesis 1:28). Before there was sin, there was law. The law given to Israel at Mount Sinai particularizes the law given in creation—and this law is best seen as a guide for Israel's vocation in the world, with a special concern for the poor and the needy. Hence, for Israel, God's redemption at the Red Sea is not an end in itself; salvation does not consist in being ushered into a time of rest and relaxation. Salvation leads to vocation in the wilderness and beyond. And that new life may entail much suffering and difficulty.

This creational basis of law is illustrated in the wilderness stories before the developments at Mount Sinai. In Exodus 18, for example, the non-Israelite Jethro, Moses's father-in-law, provides Moses with good counsel regarding social and judicial structures. This text recognizes the importance of natural law—that is, law that is available to those who stand, like Jethro, outside the chosen community. Such law is understood as a gift of God's creational activity. The natural law present in Exodus 18 leads to the revelation of law at Mount Sinai (Exodus 20–24) and, thereby, the giving of law for the chosen people.

The law in the Pentateuch is not presented in the form of a law code; the law does not stand alone as law. Rather, law is interwoven with the ongoing story of Israel's life in the wilderness. There is a rhythm in these texts: story, law, story, law. Much of Israel's law emerges over the course of the story of their wilderness experience, from Exodus to Deuteronomy. Law is always intersecting with Israel's life story and the related narrative, and it is filled with contingency and change, with complexity and ambiguity. New statutes and other divine words enjoin Israel all along the way. So God's will for God's people is not delivered to them in a once-and-for-all fashion. The will of God is a dynamic reality, intersecting with life and all of its contingencies; hence, there is clearly presented in the text itself an ongoing revision of law. Such a revisional process can even be particularly observed in the detailed repetition and change of the Ten Commandments between Exodus 20 and Deuteronomy 5. Inasmuch as God is the author of Israel's law, something like this must

> God's will for God's people is not delivered to them in a once-and-for-all fashion.

be said in view of these changes in the law: *God revises God* for the sake of the changing community of God's people.

The image of wilderness helps us understand the basic character of law. On the one hand, the law provides something of a compass for life, for wandering in the wilderness. On the other hand, the contingencies of wilderness wandering keep the law from becoming absolutized in a once-for-all form. Law in and of itself tends to promote a myth of certainty, suggesting that God's will for every aspect of life is the same in every time and place. Actual life, however, especially when seen from the perspective of the wilderness, is filled with changing circumstances in which nothing on the ship of life seems to be tied down. This means that new laws will be needed, and older laws will need to be revised, or perhaps put on the back shelf. God will speak new words of law in view of life's ongoing twists and turns. New occasions teach new duties. Such changes in the law take place because God's will in giving the law is fundamentally gracious, concerned with the life, health, and well-being of an ever-changing community and each individual therein. The changing law functions as a dynamic reality within a community on the move; the law will not stand still any more than the community will.

And so, using earlier language, the image of wilderness as narrated in these texts lifts up a basic principle for understanding the will of God for all relationships: constancy and change. Law takes ongoing experience into account while remaining constant in its objective: the best life for as many as possible. God gives the law "so that you may live, and that it may go well with you, and that you may live long in the land that you are to possess" (Deuteronomy 5:33). The law is a gracious gift of God, offered for the best interests of the ever-changing community.

Both constancy and change are basic to law because they are basic to life. Internal tensions and inconsistencies in these laws are not ironed out. Old law and new law remain side by side, not unlike a modern lawyer's library, as a canonical witness to the process of unfolding law in view of new times and places.

Hence, development in the law is just as canonical as are individual laws or the body of law as a whole. Instead of an immutable, timeless law, the text witnesses to a developing process in which experience in every sphere of life is drawn into the orbit of law (compare to motor vehicle laws or tax laws today). This ongoing formulation of new and/or revised laws is in tune with God's intention. Some of those laws may stand over against existing biblical statutes, but this development in the law should take place only after a thorough and careful examination of existing law. How to sort out constancy and change with respect to the development of law is, of course, one big question that needs ongoing consideration. The reality of ever-changing law recognizes God's ever-changing will in view of an ever-changing world.

As I get out and about in religious communities, I am alarmed at the extent to which the will of God comes into the conversation, perhaps especially in thinking about issues of evil and suffering. It seems people often believe that the will of God is unchanging and irresistible; whatever God wills, God gets done. And this perspective regarding God's will creates all sorts of dissonance in ever-changing religious communities, recognized or not.

If God's will is always accomplished in the world, then—to think of the human breaking of commandments, which are an expression of the will of God—just how does that idea work? Or, from another angle, if God's will is always accomplished, then why does God ever get angry (over six hundred references in the Bible)? God would then have to be angry at God's own self! Again and again, the biblical texts claim that human beings can successfully resist the will of God and that God gets angry because of that creaturely reality. God does not always get God's will done in the world, most especially because of human resistance. Recall Jesus's words over Jerusalem: "How often have I desired to gather your children together as a hen gathers her brood under her wings, and you were not willing!" (Matthew 23:37).

> God does not always get God's will done in the world, most especially because of human resistance.

The will of God also comes into play in the phrase used by Jesus, "not my will, but yours be done" (Luke 22:42). We often attach that phrase to our prayers, not least of all at times when we experience suffering and death. That dimension of prayer can be appropriate in certain situations, but it should not be used if it could be misunderstood by persons present that *whatever happens* is the will of God. Several years ago, a student talked about hearing that phrase in a prayer at the bedside of her very sick three-year-old child. Some family members who heard that prayer concluded that whatever happened to the child, whether she lived or died, was the will of God—apparently because they believed that God's will always gets done. At times, it seems, such an understanding of the will of God may be fostered by a lot of religious talk. I think this reality is one of the more common reasons so many people—young and old—get turned off by the church and its teachings.

A commonly used phrase regarding the issue of suffering in some religious circles runs like this: God will not give you more than you can handle. Well, the assumption—that whatever happens to you in the journey of life is the will of God—will not do. *God* may not give you more than you can handle, but the Hitlers of this world will certainly do so! And God has chosen to relate to this kind of world in such a way that much pain and suffering may be an integral part of ongoing life.

9

For the Good of All

God so enters into relationships that God will be active in the life of the world.

God is present and active in all creation. Such an understanding is supported by many scriptural texts. God "[fills] heaven and earth" (Jeremiah 23:24; see Psalm 139). God is part of the map of reality and is in relationship with all that is not God. The earth is also "full of the steadfast love of the Lord" (Psalm 33:5; see also 36:5). God is not simply here and there; God is always *lovingly* present, in every divine act, whether of judgment or salvation. Hence, God's presence is not static or passive; it is profoundly grounded in and informed by steadfast love and also working for the good of all, even in the midst of judgment.

The numerous active verbs of which God is the subject demonstrate that Israel's God is an acting God; indeed, God is active in every event (though not with the same intensity). No *full* account of any event in the life of the world is possible without factoring God's activity into it. Such divine activity includes God's word; no wedge should be driven between a speaking God and an acting God. At the same time, God's intense or special presence is associated with certain times and places (e.g., tabernacle, Exodus 40:34–38) and with the chosen people (Exodus 29:45–46). According to Psalm 104:1–4:

> God is not simply here and there; God is always *lovingly* present, in every divine act.

> O Lord my God, you are very great.
> You are clothed with honor and majesty,
>   wrapped in light as with a garment.
> You stretch out the heavens like a tent,
>   you set the beams of your chambers on the waters,
> you make the clouds your chariot,
>   you ride on the wings of the wind,
> you make the winds your messengers,
>   fire and flame your ministers.

God has made this world an integral part of God's very own dwelling place. The result, to use the language of Isaiah 66:1, is that heaven is God's throne and the earth is God's footstool. Hence, as already noted, any movement of God from heaven to earth or from earth to heaven is simply a movement from one part of the created order to another. God—who is other than world—works from within the world, not on the world from without (as if a resident of another world).

Scholarly focus on history or on decisive events in that history has tended to focus on a narrower range of God's activity. While God's acting is focused in Israel, and God's speaking is especially articulate there, the divine activity is not limited either to Israel's life or to historical events. Genesis 1–11, for example, portrays a God whose *universal, pre-Israelite* activity includes creating, grieving, judging, saving, electing, promising, blessing, covenant-making, and law-giving. That "global" portrayal of God introduces the God of Israel and shapes how one should understand the pervasive presence of that God. God's actions in and for Israel thus occur *within* God's more comprehensive ways of acting in the larger world and are shaped by God's overarching purposes for that world. Other texts reinforce the understanding that even God's salvific actions, as well as a knowledge of God, are not confined to Israel or effected only through Israel's mediation. For example, Amos 9:7:

> Are you not like the Ethiopians to me,
>> O people of Israel? says the Lord.
> Did I not bring Israel up from the land of Egypt,
>> and the Philistines from Caphtor and the
>>> Aramaeans from Kir?

In addition to the text's frequent witness to the pervasiveness of God's activity in the world, it reveals numerous other dimensions of that work.

God's Purposes

God's actions are *always purposeful* and not idle or accidental. Every divine act is an act of will and always stands in the service of God's purposes in the world. God's speaking, for example, represents a decision by God to activate God's will in a given situation. This divine word does not make God present but seeks to clarify and direct God's personal will within God's already pervasive presence. Every divine action is informed by God's ultimate salvific will for the world, by God's faithfulness to promises made, and by God's steadfast love for all.

Distinctions within the will of God are textually recognized. On the one hand, God's will for salvation is absolute and ultimate (e.g., Genesis 12:3: "in you all the families of the earth shall be blessed"). On the other hand, God's will for judgment is contingent and circumstantial, and always stands in the service of God's salvific will (e.g., Jeremiah 26:2–3):

> Thus says the Lord: Stand in the court of the Lord's house, and speak to all the cities of Judah that come to worship in the house of the Lord; speak to them all the words that I command you; do not hold back a word. It may be that they will listen, all of them, and will turn from their evil way, that I may change my mind about the disaster that I intend to bring on them because of their evil doings.

Unlike divine love, divine wrath is not an attribute intrinsic to God, because if there were no sin, there would be no wrath.[1]

God's Discernment

God's acting in the world's life is always *situationally appropriate*, fitting for specific times and places. God's "seeing" is often said to precede the divine acting (Exodus 3:7–10; cf. 2:24–25). God is a master at discernment, seeing what is needed in a given situation and acting in a way that fits the needs of that moment. God's actions are always related to particular situations in the world and are designed to make a difference in that situation. At the same time, within those focused actions, God has the more comprehensive divine purposes in view (e.g., Exodus 9:16: "But this is why I have let you live: to show you my power, and to make my name resound through all the earth.").

> God is a master at discernment, seeing what is needed in a given situation and acting in a way that fits the needs of that moment.

Using Exodus 1–15 to illustrate, we see that God's actions in this time and place are related to the specifics of Israel's slavery. Hence, God does not respond to human oppression of a sociopolitical sort by ignoring those realities. At this point, God acts to save Israel not from its own sins, but from the negative effects of the sins of others. God's saving actions in connection with the return from exile, however, have different needs of Israel in view; Israel is forgiven its sin and saved from the effects of its own sinfulness (see Isaiah 43:25; 40:1–11).

God's Effectiveness

God's activity is *effective* in the world, from the creating of the world, to the deliverance of Israel from Egypt, to judgment on Israel by various foreign armies. God *does* get things done in the world. At the same time, as noted, given God's ways of working, God's work in the world is not always successful.

Two comprehensive outcomes of God's work in the world might be noted. For one, God's actions issue in *new knowledge* of God and of God's purposes in the world. New promises are stated, new responsibilities are delineated, and religious issues are clarified and judged. Given the ongoing experiential character of "knowing" for Israel, this divine action affects not simply head knowledge, but the entire relationship between the knower and the known. The importance of verbal events for the development of such new knowledge should be highlighted more than has commonly been the case. Meaning is not simply inferred from historical events. For example, God's verbal encounter with Moses at the burning bush (see Exodus 3:1–6) gives Moses the capacity to see the "something more" in the events, and the events' actual occurrence confirms and fills out that knowledge.

God's actions also issue in *a becoming*. Divine actions have to do not simply with matters of revelation; God's actions *effect* a new relationship with God and a changed status for human beings and communities (for example, freedom from oppression). God also acts to this end in and through various forms of Israel's worship life. The dramatized festivals (Passover, Weeks, Tabernacles, and others) are considered by participants to be vehicles for God's ongoing salvific activity among the people. In other words, God's saving activity in historical events is made newly available to Israel in these liturgical events. As an example, Israel's sacrificial system has a sacramental structure in and through which God acts to forgive the penitent worshiper. Israel's worship constitutes an important matrix for Israel's becoming as well as for the reception of new knowledge of the God who acts therein.

God's Knowledge

Though not as commonly recognized as it should be, God's actions may also issue in new knowledge and becoming *for God*. Human responses to God's actions may lead to a new level of *divine* knowing (see Genesis 22:12, "*now* I [God] know," and Deuteronomy 8:2, "testing you to know"—that is, "so I [God] may know"). This development in God's knowledge can lead to new directions in divine action. (See the several possible futures *for God* in view of human-divine interaction in, for example, Jeremiah 22:1–5.)

Note also the use of the language of a divine "if" and a divine "perhaps" regarding the relationship.[2] The divine "perhaps" (or "it may be"), stated several times in the prophets (Ezekiel 12:1–3; Jeremiah 26:2–3; 36:3, 7; 51:8; Isaiah 47:12), suggests a level of divine uncertainty on God's part as to how the people will respond to the prophetic word. Comparably, see the divine "if" in Jeremiah 22:4–5:

> For if you will indeed obey this word, then through the gates of this house shall enter kings who sit on the

throne of David, riding in chariots and on horses, they, and their servants, and their people. But if you will not heed these words, I swear by myself, says the Lord, that this house shall become a desolation.

Two specific future possibilities are open to the king (and to the people—Jeremiah 22:2), depending upon whether justice is fulfilled according to the command of the Lord (see 22:3–5). For each of these options to have integrity, it is necessary for God not to know what will in fact happen—namely, that the negative judgment will be exacted. If the positive future of Jeremiah 22:4b is a genuine possibility for the king, then for God as well it must be a possibility, and, finally, only a *possibility*.

> New experiences for God have an effect on the life and thought of God.

New commitments made by God and new relationships established by God with creatures (such as in the wake of a call from God to a new vocation) change the divine life. In some sense, in view of such texts, one must speak of *newness* for God as well. This newness can thus be said to be prompted by God's ongoing new experiences of the world's life. God can know novelty, and such new experiences for God have an effect on the life and thought of God.

God and the Extraordinary

While all of God's activities are related to worldly situations in a meaningful way, some divine actions *are more significant than others.* (See the examples of such differences in divine actions that are lifted up in texts such as Deuteronomy 16:1–17; 26:5–9.) These more significant divine actions may be, but are not necessarily, related to the events being *extraordinary or miraculous.* Where these kinds of elements do occur in the texts, they are not easily sorted out or interpreted.

The extraordinariness of divine action is not necessarily understood in terms of divine intervention or intrusion, as if God were normally not present and then "intervenes" at certain moments to make things happen. God is present on every occasion and active in every event. While God is likely understood to act in the world in and through the means of cause and effect provided by the world, sufficient "play" exists in that continuum to allow for God to work and for the unusual event to take place.

Still, the language used for, say, the exodus events includes extraordinary features, from the plagues to the Passover epidemic to the sea crossing. Isaiah 40–55 also uses extraordinary images to speak of Israel's future return from exile (including changes in the natural order: e.g., Isaiah 41:18–20), and these texts link this extraordinariness to God's new work. Yet, the fall of Jerusalem and the return of the exiles are described in the more mundane terms of Babylonian army movements and Persian royal policies. This distinction between the event itself and the rhetoric of extraordinariness regarding the divine action is different from the exodus account, where they are integrated. A liturgical setting for the exodus complex of events (cf. the Passover in Exodus 12) may inform and heighten the dramatic character of the telling. These texts have to do with actions of God, but the function of the texts' extraordinary features may have to do more with rhetorical strategy and liturgical drama than with literal description, not dissimilar to the rhetoric used by the texts in Deutero-Isaiah.

The extraordinariness in Deutero-Isaiah's testimony regarding Israel's return from exile need not literally describe Israel's actual history in order to speak the truth about God's acts and for it to be theologically and religiously significant. Yet, if no links exist between the confession regarding God's activity and Israel's life, at least in its broad strokes, then the confession becomes problematic. The "happenedness" of those events that Israel has confessionally interpreted as *constitutive* of its identity is indispensable for faith, even if they cannot finally be verified or spelled out in detail. But divine activity should be linked not only to the events themselves but also to the confessional activity that interprets them. These realities belong together in any statement about the God who acts; only God's act comprehended through the gift of faith enables the confession that God has acted in Israel's external world (see Exodus 14:31 and the Song of Moses that follows in Exodus 15).

God is not the only agent associated with certain of the extraordinary events that the text presents. Both human and nonhuman agents are engaged. In the plagues, for example, divine agency is explicitly associated with only six plagues (1, 4, 5, 7, 8, 10). Aaron/Moses are involved in three of these plagues in a dual role (1, 7, 8), and a nonhuman agent is cited in the eighth plague. In four of the plague texts, only human agency is cited (2, 3, 6, 9). Both God and Israel recognize this dual agency

(Exodus 3:8–10; 14:31), but the texts do not factor out just how this duality works.[3]

Efforts have been made to explain the extraordinary elements in these texts in natural terms. For example, in the plague stories, the frogs leave bloody water, flies are drawn to dead frogs, etc. The gifts of manna, quail, and water in the wilderness have also been so interpreted. Such reflections need not "explain away" the divine factor, however, if God is kept in the picture (which is not always done). Consideration of divine providence should not be divorced from recognition of nature's God-given potentialities.

To cite one example, see the action of God in the "water from the rock" incident reported in Exodus 17:1–7. God is here not creating water out of thin air, nor is nature disrupted by some divine miracle. Water does course through rock formations; the actions of both God and Moses enable their hidden potential to surface. God works in and through the natural (and the human) to provide water for the people, as God does throughout the complex of events that make up the exodus.

The Intensity of God's Presence

God acts differently in some events. How to articulate this difference is difficult, but it may be due to variations in the *intensification* of divine action. In some texts, God's presence is more unobtrusive (for instance, God never is said to appear to Joseph or his brothers in Genesis 37–50, yet God is an effective agent, evident explicitly in Genesis 50:20). In other texts, God's presence is more intense (e.g., Exodus 40:34–38). In developing a typology of divine presence, one might speak of variations in intensification, perhaps including categories such as God's general presence, God's accompanying presence, God's tabernacling presence, and God's theophanic presence.[4]

These distinctions no doubt relate to the needs of the situation and God's purposes related thereto. One might also speak about God's concern for human life and freedom in the face of too sustained a divine intensity. Recall the claim that one cannot see God and live (Exodus 33:20).[5] But such differences also involve the dynamics of the God-world relationship and God's related commitments. For example, God's promise at the end of the flood story never to act in that way again (stated in both Genesis 8:21–22 and 9:11) limits the divine options (see my earlier discussion of divine self-limitation) with respect to any related matter. One could say something comparable about divine self-limitation with respect to all of God's promises, for God will keep those promises, come what may.

Or the intensity of the divine presence may be affected by the depths of human sinfulness. So, for example, God is *driven* from the temple by Israel's abominations (Ezekiel 8:6), and Israel's iniquities, the prophet says, "have made a separation between you and your God" (Isaiah 59:2 ESV). Negative human responses can push God back along the continuum of presence (it is assumed that God's activity is not irresistible) so that God's presence becomes less intense and, hence, less felt and effective. Positively, human need and powerlessness may call forth intensity in God's presence (see Deuteronomy 32:36; God acts when "he sees that their power is gone"). God's possibilities are closely related to the nature and intensity of the worldly situation. For a variety of reasons God does act differently in events, but the reader cannot finally sort out the factors that are at work within these differences.

In sum, the present and active God is at work in the world within committed relationships in accordance with the divine will. God's actions are always appropriate for the situation, and they effect new creaturely knowledge and becoming, though that divine action in both word and deed is resistible and, hence, may not always be successful (a divine reality that is not as sufficiently recognized as it should be). God acts directly through various means, both human and nonhuman, so that not only is the world dependent upon God, but God has also chosen to be dependent on the world. God's actions may be of varying intensities, and some acts are more significant than others, but their import is not necessarily related to the extraordinariness of events.

> Not only is the world dependent upon God, but God has also chosen to be dependent on the world.

10

An Element of Uncertainty

God so enters into relationships that God recognizes the need for a healthy "space" between those who are in relationship.

We all know that in relationships with others (think of parents and their children, or spouses), individuals can be or get too close; we can be too present to one another. This commonly experienced interhuman reality raises a question about the nature of the God-human relationship: Can *God* be too close or get too close to us? Yes! Too direct a divine presence to individuals or communities would annul human life as a flame kills a butterfly.

Whatever the intensification of God's presence may be in any given time or place, there must be an element of ambiguity or uncertainty for human beings regarding the identity of the

God in whom they believe. God's presence cannot be obvious, or it would be coercive; if that were the case, faith would be turned into sight and humankind could not but believe. God must set people at a certain distance from God; whatever the intensification of divine presence, there must be an element of uncertainty regarding the divine identity. God so enters into relationship with human beings that God must give them space to be themselves—with all the risks that that involves.

> God so enters into relationship with human beings that God must give them space to be themselves.

These observations raise the question of structural (or epistemic) presence, perhaps best evident in the sentence "No one shall see [God] and live" (Exodus 33:20). This distance is a reality that God has structured into the created order for the purpose of preserving human freedom, indeed human life. For God to be fully present to human beings would be coercive.[1]

11

The Gift of Prayer

God so enters into relationships that God is not the only
one who has something important to say.

Communication is key to a healthy relationship in the human
sphere; that reality is also true with respect to the God-
human relationship. And so, in the interests of that relationship,
the Old Testament often speaks of
prayer, of communication between
God and human—from complaint
to praise, from lament to intercession. Indeed, prayer could be said to
be God's gift for the sake of a healthy
relationship. And God takes such
conversations seriously.

> Prayer could be
> said to be God's
> gift for the sake
> of a healthy
> relationship.

For example, during the wilderness wanderings, what people have to say to God plays an important role in the development of the God-human relationship. One first notes the song of praise in Exodus 15. Israel offers its praise to God for all that God has done for them in their deliverance from enslavement in Egypt. Praise is voiced at the beginning of the wilderness journey and shapes Israel's ongoing life in that often forlorn, even dangerous setting.

The praise of God must be considered from at least two perspectives: Praise is a word *to* God, in thanks for all that God has done on Israel's behalf. Praise is also a word *about* God, voiced in a public way as a testimony to all who would hear, that, even in the wilderness, this God is a God of salvation.

But then, in view of ongoing troubles, praise turns to complaint. Even with the memory of salvation at the Red Sea close at hand, distrust and rebellion can rear their ugly heads. Any wilderness journey will include such moments or even periods of crisis that are rife with difficulties and dangers, from agents both human and nonhuman. Wilderness life is full of ongoing insecurity, with uncertainty regarding the future. Even slavery back in Egypt can begin to look attractive by comparison (as noted in Exodus 14:11–12).

Certain texts even picture God in agony over the absence of prayer on the part of God's rebellious people. See the divine testimony in Isaiah 65:1 (ESV, variant in note): "I was ready to be sought by those who did not ask for me; I was ready to be found by those who did not seek me. I said, 'Here I am, here I am,' to a nation that did not call upon my name." When God's people do not pray, it hurts God. Even in the absence of prayer, God remains eager for communication (Isaiah 65:2). It is important to note, however, that such complaints and laments are freely voiced. Israel speaks its mind to God, and God hears. One might question the complaining tone, but the fact that Israel openly voices its complaints to God is an important recognition of the character of the ongoing relationship between Israel and Israel's God. What people have to say, even in rebellious times, counts with God![1]

> If God wants mature followers, the possibility of their defiance must be risked.

Israel's time in the wilderness is finally shaped by God's extraordinary patience and mercy, and by God's will to stay with the people on this journey. Coping with this complaining and idolatrous people is no easy task, even for God. No divine flick of the wrist is capable of straightening them out without compromising their freedom. If God wants mature followers, the possibility of their defiance must be risked.

And defiance does arise. The people's complaining takes a turn toward rebellion. In Exodus 32–34, chapters that are placed between tabernacle planning and tabernacle building, is the story of the construction of the golden calf. Israel becomes impatient with Moses and God and turns to idolatry—to a type of god that can be seen and touched. Wilderness is also a place of temptation, where in view of various troubles and where God seems absent from life, one might turn to easy and visible forms of deity. For example, one might turn to thinking about a god who can be brought under control by human words and actions and harnessed to do whatever the pray-er wants done.

God is genuinely affected by this rebellious, complaining turn on Israel's part, and so deeply that God considers severely disciplining Israel and starting all over again with Moses (Exodus 32:9–10). But Moses intercedes on behalf of Israel, and God hears his prayer and reverses the decision. In his intercession, Moses does not suggest that God's judgment is inappropriate. Nor does Moses appeal to Israel's good deeds as something that God should take into account, nor does he give God data of which God was previously unaware. Moses's reasons for God to show mercy are threefold (see Exodus 32): the nature of God's actions in recent events (in view of those divine actions, what sense does punishment make?); God's reputation among the nations (what will "the neighbors" say?); and God's promises ("God, you promised!").

How persuasive are these arguments for God? Most significant in the situation for God is that certain matters are being forcefully articulated by one with whom God has established a close relationship. Moses does not win an argument with God, but because God so values the relationship with Moses, his prayer changes the decision-making situation (for both God and Moses). God is now open and willing to change directions in moving into the future. The new energy and insight that Moses brings into the moment changes the dynamics of the situation with which God has to work. God has some new ingredients with which to work and some new directions to take. God takes the response of the other in the relationship with genuine seriousness. The result is that God responds to Moses's prayers: "And the Lord changed his mind about the disaster that he planned to bring on his people" (Exodus 32:14). What Moses prays has an effect on God. In view of the nature of the God-human relationship, prayers can give a different shape to the future, both for God and human and for their interrelationship. What believers have to say counts with God (in every generation!) and can open up new possibilities for both divine action and human action in the situation.

Prayer and God's Promises

The people of God have been gifted with the power of prayer as a means through which they can make a situation more open for God and the mission of God can be furthered in the life of the world—even beyond the range of our voices. Prayer is a God-given way for God's people to give God more room to work, knowing that God always has our best interests at heart. As such, this God is revealed not as one who is unbending or unyielding, nor as one who assumes a "take it or leave it" attitude in the situation. The people of God are not in the hands of an iron fate or a predetermined order of things. God is open to

> Prayer is a God-given way for God's people to give God more room to work, knowing that God always has our best interests at heart.

taking new directions in life in view of new times and places; God is open to changing the divine course of action in view of the interaction within the relationship, including our prayers. Yet, never changing will be God's steadfast love for all, God's saving will for everyone, and God's faithfulness to promises made. God keeps promises.

For example, hear these thoughts reflected in 2 Kings 20:1–7. God through the prophet Isaiah tells King Hezekiah that he will die. Then Hezekiah prays, reminding God of his faithfulness, and weeps. Then God tells Isaiah that Hezekiah's prayer has been heard, that he would be healed, and that the people would be delivered from the Assyrians. God, who initially speaks a word of judgment to Hezekiah ("you shall die; you shall not recover," v. 1), so values Hezekiah's prayer in response that God reverses a divine decision: "I have heard your prayer, I have seen your tears; indeed, I will heal you" (v. 5).

Reflecting this Old Testament understanding, in our church practice we commonly teach people—I'm thinking especially of faithful Christian people—that prayer to God is important and that prayer really does have the potential to change things. We teach that petitionary prayer and intercessory prayer are important Christian practices. And we certainly often make it sound in our theological rhetoric as if God might be actually influenced by our prayers and respond to what we have to say.

But we often discourage an active prayer life on the part of many people by the way in which we speak about the God to whom we pray. We often teach, implicitly or explicitly, that God cannot be moved by any human action, that God certainly cannot be persuaded by anything human beings have to say, that God will do what God will do regardless of what we have to say. We claim that God has given prayer to us as a gift to encourage communication between ourselves and God. Yet, all too often we convey the idea that while prayer may bring us closer to God, prayer does not actually have an effect on God. In the process, our understanding of the relationship with God may diminish in depth and breadth. As a result, the efficacy of prayer may often be considered very limited indeed, and that understanding will finally discourage people from praying in any serious way.

A footnote may be suggested. In speaking about God's responses to prayer we tend to overuse the word "answer"; we thereby encourage people to look for God's responses to their prayers in ways that bear a precise relation to their requests. So, if a given post-prayer situation does not look exactly like our request, we too often conclude God has not answered our prayers or has said no to them. Then we either blame God for what has happened or blame ourselves for not speaking correctly to God or having enough faith in God or the like, as if there are no other possible interpretations—such as, for example, that God's will in responding to our prayers was successfully resisted by a person or situation. Indeed, one key factor that needs to be taken into consideration is the pervasiveness of sin and evil in everyday life. Given the nature of the relationship, such (common!) realities can get in the way of God's responses to our prayers.

Consider a situation in which we pray to God for healing, but healing is not forthcoming. When that happens, we may end up blaming God for not answering our prayers or wondering why God did not answer our prayers. We so often make God "the heavy" in these matters. In fact, however, the problem may have been the medicine we were taking or not taking; it may have been a member of the medical community with whom we were working who had had too much to drink the night before the surgery. Any number of other human failings could be cited that have the potential for giving a negative shape to the life situation. Sometimes when we pray, we may think all that is at work in this situation is our prayer and God. But a multitude of other factors are commonly present in any given moment. Some of those realities may be so resistant to God's will in one situation or another that God's will for us does not get done. And God's heart is the first heart to break; God's tears are the first to flow.

In thinking about God and prayer, we should use wording such as that God "responds" rather than God "answers." That language would better enable people to think about God's involvement in their lives without always looking for an answer so specific that they miss seeing the various ways in which God is actually responding. The divine-human interaction is genuine conversation and has a fundamental integrity to it. Not only does what God says affect the relationship; what human beings say affects the relationship as well. God so enters into relationships that God is not the only one who has something important to say or do.

> In thinking about God and prayer, we should use wording such as that God "responds" rather than God "answers."

12

Sharing Power

God so enters into relationships that God is not the only one who has something important to do and the power with which to do it.

Within the very creative process itself, God chooses to share power with the creatures, both nonhuman (e.g., Genesis 1:11–13, 20, 22, 24) and human (Genesis 1:26, 28). The first word from God to the newly created human beings, "Be fruitful and multiply, and fill the earth and subdue it" (Genesis 1:28), is a power-sharing move, and that kind of relationship between God and both humans and nonhuman continues in the post-creation world (e.g., Psalm 65:12–13; Haggai 1:10–11; Psalm 8). This God chooses to share power and responsibility with that which is other than God, to exercise constraint and restraint in the use of power in the world ("I will never again . . .

nor will I ever again . . . ," Genesis 8:21–22), and to honor promises made, even to the point of placing God's own life on the line (Genesis 15:7–21).

Think about relationship and the exercise of power. The language of omnipotence often enters into conversations about God's power. Such language has been a prominent part of the church's classical understanding of God. I think that such language can still be used. The question at stake is not whether God is all-powerful; the issue is the nature of God's *exercise* of power in view of the committed relationship. Doesn't genuine relationship mean that both parties to the relationship not only share power, but exercise constraint and restraint in their *use* of power? Love always qualifies the use of power. God chooses to entrust us with tasks and responsibilities, and one thing that decision means is that God will not intervene to "fix" things every time they are being misused. What a lousy parent I would be if I stepped in to fix things every time my children messed up! And children will spot that kind of parenting a mile away. Does not genuine relationship mean that God will enter into situations of interdependence so that humans are not simply dependent and God simply independent (see Romans 10:14–15)? We would certainly want to allow God the freedom to limit the exercise of power for

> The question at stake is not whether God is all-powerful; the issue is the nature of God's *exercise* of power in view of the committed relationship.

the sake of the relationship (one thinks of self-limitation in inter-human relationships). God has made promises, and because God is faithful to commitments made, God will not suspend these commitments to get something done. This is a divine act of self-limitation, which God will honor.

The language of control is also often used for God in this kind of context, and the idea is out and about in bumper sticker verbiage: "God is in control."[1] But is not this type of language overly ambiguous? What does "control" mean—crowd control, mind control, absolute control, a controlling personality? If we make the unqualified claim that God is in control of the other in a relationship, then the relationship must be less than genuine. Let's ask, Where was God in the experience of 9/11? If God is in control, then God was in control of those planes heading into the World Trade Center. If that was the case, was this violence God's will? Or was God's will being successfully resisted? Did God try to stop the attack but failed? Or take natural disasters: Is God in control of such events? At least with respect to some natural disasters (Hurricane Katrina, for instance), claiming that God is in control seems a remarkably "easy" way of discounting human failure.

A brief aside: One helpful response to issues relating to God's use of power on 9/11 is that of Lewis B. Smedes: "For me there was no mystery about where God was and what God was up to on the morning of September 11, 2001. God was right there doing what God always does in the presence of evil that is willed by humans—fighting it, resisting it, battling it, trying God's best to keep it from happening. This time evil won. God, we hope, will one day emerge triumphant over evil—though, on the way to that glad day, God sometimes takes a beating."[2] This is a thoughtful reflection, though I wish Smedes had added the phrase "like Jesus did on the cross."

To (seek to) be in control of the other in a relationship is to participate in a relationship that lacks integrity, even for God. This imaging of God as one who is "in control" has some sharp implications for the shape of the church and the life of faith. If God is in control, then, by definition, this will become something of a pattern for human activity. We are created in the image of God, and such an understanding would mean we are created in the image of an all-controlling God. For example, with respect to the environment, the implication could easily be drawn that because we are in control of it, we can do whatever we please with it.

> To (seek to) be in control of the other in a relationship is to participate in a relationship that lacks integrity, even for God.

Power-related language includes words such as "let" and "allow." The use of these words with God as subject is quite common, particularly in response to tragedy, suffering, or the experience of evil: God *let* this tragedy occur; God *allowed* the death of this child to happen. And if people think carefully about the implications of using that language for God in such an indiscriminate way, or perhaps even soak it up without thinking about it much, then they could reason: Let's see, if God made a decision to allow a specific instance of suffering, that means God could've stopped it but chose not to do so. At the end of the day, the folks who are suffering (or those close to them) might well conclude that to say God allowed a child to die is no different from saying God caused the child's death. *God* is the one responsible for the suffering or the death that has been experienced. And as a result, all too commonly I hear from people: I don't want anything to do with that kind of God, or, more softly, I'm not going to take such a God seriously.

Is the language of allowance then of no use at all? It can be used in appropriate ways, but one has to be careful with how it is used. That is, it is not helpful to speak of God's "allowing" specific events, as if God were making specific decisions to let certain events occur: this, that, but not that! I think the only helpful way one can use this kind of language is to talk about divine commitments. God has made commitments to the creation that it will *be allowed* to be what it was created to be. That conviction would include events from the procreation of human beings to natural disasters and their ill effects upon creatures involved.

God's Work through Agents

Key to understanding God's use of power is this fact: God works through human language and various human and nonhuman agents (violent and nonviolent) to get things done in the world. God acts directly, but always through means. And the variety of means is impressive. From the beginning, God works in and through that which is already created to bring about new creations (e.g., Genesis 1:2, 11, 20, 24); God works to call Abraham through human language, as well as through Abraham's inter-rupted journey to Canaan (Genesis 11:31–12:3). God works through nonhuman agents in the plagues, at Passover, and at the Red Sea (the nonhuman is imaged as the savior of the human!). God works in and through the sacrificial rituals to bring about the forgiveness of sin and reconciliation with God as well. God works in and through the prophets to speak God's word of judg-ment and grace. God works in and through the continuing moral order—a loose causal weave of act and consequence, which can be named the judgment of God.

God's use of—even dependence on!—human agents in both judgment and salvation is especially prominent. For exam-ple, God works through non-chosen, non-Israelite kings and armies to send Israel into exile and to bring them home again, amply demonstrated in texts such as Isaiah 10:5 ("Assyria, the rod of my anger") and Isaiah 45:1 (God's "anointed" in this text is King Cyrus of Persia). God even refers to the Babylonian monarch Nebuchadnezzar as "my servant" (Jeremiah 25:9; 27:6; 43:10). In such divine activity, creaturely agency is not reduced to impotence. God's activity is not all-determining; what non-divine agents do and say makes a difference in the historical process. God neither "lets go" of the creation nor retains all power in the various situations of life. Both God and creatures are effective agents.

Because God does not perfect human beings (or other crea-tures), with all their foibles and flaws, before deciding to work in and through them, God's actions through them will always have mixed results. God works with what is available, including the institutions of society; among such institutions in that ancient context were certain ways of waging war and other trappings of government. More generally, violence will *inevitably* be associated with God's work in the world because, to a greater or lesser degree, violence is characteristic of the persons and institutions and other agents in and through which that work of God is done. Hence, such work by the agents will always have varied results and will be less positive than what would have happened had God chosen to act alone. It may be said that much, if not all, of the violence and other negative effects associated with God's actions in, say, the exodus events (and more generally in the Bible) is due to God's decision to work in and through agents who are capable of violence.

> Because God does not perfect human beings (or other creatures), with all their foibles and flaws, God's actions through them will always have mixed results.

God does not (micro)manage the work of the agents but exercises constraint and restraint in relating to them and their activities. This point is demonstrated, as noted above, by texts that show that God's agents, in their use of power, may exceed the divine mandate, going beyond anything God intended, and complicate God's work on Israel's behalf. The agents of God are not puppets in the hand of God! Agents can misuse the power they have been given by God. They can act in ways that fly in the face of the will of God (to which the wrath of God is responsive). Hence, the will and purpose of God, indeed the sovereignty of God, active in these events is not "irresistible." God has chosen not to be the only agent at work in the world, nor has God chosen to be all-controlling in work with individual or corporate agents.

Harsh words are used with God as subject because they depict the actions of those in and through whom God mediates judgment. The text portrays God's violent actions in conformity to the means God uses. One cannot conclude from this observation that God is never associated with violent activity. Because God has determined to work in and through agents that are capable of violence, God's work in the world will always have both potential and actual violent dimensions.

For these reasons, interpreters must not diminish the distinction between God and God's agents or discount the very real power of these human armies. God uses the means available in that particular time and place, but God does not necessarily condone the violent means in and through which God works. A helpful example is Zechariah 1:15, "I am extremely angry with the nations that are at ease; for while I was only a little angry, they made the disaster worse." This divine decision to work in and through such (potentially) violent means is a risky move for God, because God thereby becomes closely associated with the agents' (often violent) activity. Notably, God assumes a share of the responsibility associated with that violence and takes part of the blame for using such agents.

Another risky move for God is God's use of agents in carrying out acts of judgment. Using the flood story as a resource, three dimensions of this issue are significant:

1. God acts in and through the agents of storm and flood that actually do the destruction. Water and flood are the subjects of the key verbs that occasion the disaster (Genesis 7:6, 10–12, 17–20, 24).

2. The created moral order (that is, the world works in such a way that acts have consequences) is also an agent in and through which God works judgment. Indeed, it may be said that the agents of destruction emerge from within the very nature of the corrupt situation. The words for "corruption" and "destruction" (Genesis 6:11–13) are from the same Hebrew root (*sh-ch-t*); on a continuum, *sh-ch-t* leads to *sh-ch-t*. The same Hebrew word is used to speak of human wickedness, the violence of "all flesh," and its effects on the earth.[3] This language shows that the destructive agents are *intrinsically* related to human corruption and are *used* by God rather than imposed by God from outside the dynamics of the situation.[4] Violence leads to violence. In other terms, creaturely violence has disastrous, indeed cosmic environmental effects (see, e.g., Hosea 4:1–3).[5] The words "only," "every," and "continually" in Genesis 6:5 specify the depth and breadth of the sinful human condition, out of which grows the cosmic violence that follows.

3. God's agents in this situation also include a "righteous" and "blameless" Noah. He fulfills every divine command, and his obedient human activity is sharply responsible for the salvation of a remnant of human beings and animals.

Given the risks associated with God's use of agents, we should not be surprised that God may end up regretting the work of God's own agents. Many prophetic texts speak of divine judgment on those nations that have been agents of God (Jeremiah 25:12–14; 27:6–7; 50:1–51:64; Isaiah 10:12–19; 47:1–15; Zechariah 1:15).[6] Notably, God assumes a share of the responsibility for that violence and its effects, and God will take on a certain blame for the use of such agents (see Jeremiah 42:10: "I am sorry for the disaster that have I brought upon you").[7] It appears that this divine response carries with it the sense of genuine regret on God's part; the judgment and its painful effects proved to be more severe than God had intended or perhaps even thought they would be (see, e.g., Jeremiah 3:19–20).

Human beings, then or now, do not have a perfect perception of how they are to serve as God's agents in the world. They are sinful and finite creatures. While it is difficult to evaluate the agents' perception, it is important to note that the role of divine agents is often expressed in terms of the direct speech of God. Inasmuch as direct divine speech is a rare phenomenon in the New Testament (four or five texts at best: e.g., the baptism of Jesus, Matthew 3:13–17), should we understand that recurrent direct divine speech in the Old Testament in less than literal terms? Israelite authors may have put into direct divine speech understandings they had gained through study and reflection rather than an actual hearing of God's words. And might we also say that Israel did not always fully understand? Israelites did understand themselves to be the agents of divine judgment against, for example, Canaanite wickedness (Deuteronomy

9:4–5) and understood themselves to have received a word from God to that end. Did they, however, fully and appropriately understand? Did they exceed the divine mandate not only in their action, but in the way in which they understood or interpreted it?

Consideration of God's work through human (or nonhuman) agents must steer between the two ditches of deism and determinism. God neither remains ensconced in heaven watching the world go by nor micromanages the world to "control" (a much-abused word) its every move, or that of its creatures, so that creaturely agency counts for nothing. But between these two ditches, the biblical texts do not always provide clear direction for reflection.

Hence, God's way into the future is not reduced to a simple divine decision to act, but God takes into account the dynamics of the human and natural situations. Because of God's committed relationship to the world and God's honoring of the agents in and through whom God has chosen to work, the agents retain the power to make decisions and execute policies that sometimes fly in the face of the will of God. The God active in these events is not all-controlling (as noted above, the use of the ambiguous word "control" can confuse the issue[8]). In some sense God takes the risk that the agents will do what they will with the mandate they have been given. One element of that risk is that God's name will become associated with the violence, indeed the excessive violence, of the conflict.

In sum, these perspectives regarding agency are testimony to a fundamentally *relational* understanding of the way in which

God acts in the world. Both God and the agents have crucial roles to play, and the function and effect of their spheres of activity are interrelated. God has so shaped the created order that there are overlapping spheres of interdependence, and God shares genuine responsibility with human and nonhuman beings. Moreover, God has determined not to "intervene" to make sure every little thing is done according to the will of God. God has put in place an ordered freedom in the creation, a degree of openness and unpredictability wherein God leaves room for genuine creaturely responses and decisions as these agents exercise their God-given power. Even more, God gives them such powers and responsibilities in a way that *commits* God to *a certain kind of ongoing relationship* with them, whatever developments may emerge.

The biblical text is testimony to a kind of divine activity that gives power over to the creature for the sake of a relationship of integrity. At the same time, this way of relating to people, not least the use of agents, reveals a divine vulnerability, for God opens the divine self to suffering and critique should things not go according to the divine will (and they often do not, given the nature of the agents). But God so values the relationship, and so binds the divine self to that relationship, that the relationship will continue in and through whatever suffering may come along—for both God and agents.

> God opens the divine self to suffering and critique should things not go according to the divine will.

Power and the Cross

This discussion can be helpfully related to Christological matters (to briefly bring the testaments together). The cross of Jesus constitutes the center in terms of which the Bible is finally to be interpreted. But when we speak of a theology of the cross, we all too often do so in combination with an amazingly imperious understanding of God. That is to say, we are often insufficiently Christocentric in our talk about God. We tend not to speak of the vulnerability of God or of God as one who acts in suffering ways in the world. We have a Jesus who suffers but a God who would never shed a tear. We keep Good Friday and Easter Sunday together well in our talk about Jesus, but our talk about God tends to be all Easter Sunday. We often separate the suffering of Jesus from the basic images we use for God. Indeed, at times we imply that Jesus came to save us *from* God! As a result, our talk about Jesus and God could be *experienced* by people as fundamentally disjunctive. One of the implications of such an understanding is a depreciation of the Old Testament and its God for many a Christian. We must speak as clearly as we can of the suffering of the God to whom the Old Testament bears witness (e.g., Jeremiah 8–9).

This disjunction may also manifest itself in styles of leadership. Our leadership styles are all too often more informed by an imperious understanding of God than by a cross-centered theology. We would do well to ask ourselves, Is vulnerability an integral part of our understanding of the church and its ministry? Our understanding of God will inevitably give shape to our public lives and our ministerial practice, not least because we are asked to follow this God in all we do and say.

On these matters, we do need to watch carefully for the danger of simply tailoring our portrayal of God to popular tastes. And let's admit it: the sovereign god of absolute power is often the popular preference. Ask a person on the street to describe God, and the language of (absolute) power will often be central. If we do not have a God whom we understand in terms of suffering and the cross, however, we end up with a generic god, a god who could be properly defined by anyone on the street or the devotee of virtually any religion. But such a word about God is nothing special for the church to claim or proclaim. That is no new word about God for the average person. We may not like the biblical word about a God who is vulnerable, who suffers for us, and who is supremely revealed in the person of Jesus. But that is a key word to emphasize when we speak about the God of the Bible. Our talk about God should match this understanding: *Jesus is not an exception in the life of God!*

> If we do not have a God whom we understand in terms of suffering and the cross, we end up with a generic god.

13

Both Settled and Unsettled

God so enters into relationships that the future is not all
mapped out.

I am amazed at how commonly the language of fatalism creeps
into our thinking about the future: The future is in God's
hands. God has it all mapped out, and what creatures do is
finally irrelevant. I submit that to leave the future simply in
God's hands is to denigrate human responsibility and to tempt
God. To do such a thing would be similar to the devil's temptation of Jesus (see Matthew 4:1–11): "Jump off the top of the
temple, Jesus; God will send his angels to save you from the
rocks below. Do you trust in God to take care of you or not?
Jump, Jesus, jump!" Jesus's response is sharp and direct: "No,
that would tempt God."

We certainly can and must leave the future ultimately in God's hands, but God's relationship with us is such that we are given a great deal to say about the shape of our own future *and* the future of others, including those less fortunate than we are. My preacher grandfather died of colon cancer much sooner than he should have. He refused to see a doctor; he often said that he was leaving his future in God's hands. Thinking that only God gives shape to one's future is still a very common perspective; all too often, unfortunately, it is an angle of vision to which the church has made a contribution.

Biblically centered students should have a different orientation regarding their own and others' future. The future is partly settled and partly unsettled. Partly settled, yes: there will be a new heaven and a new earth; God will raise you from the dead and grant you eternal life. But your future is also unsettled: your words and deeds with respect to, say, the less fortunate in your community, will make a difference in their future and yours; there is an openness regarding that future that leaves room for the ever-changing effects of what you do and say.

> God's relationship with us is such that we are given a great deal to say about the shape of our own future *and* the future of others.

Through being empowered by the creative gifts of God, human beings (of all ages, in different ways) are capable of giving shape to the nature of their future and the future of others.

For example, in texts such as Jeremiah 22:1–5, the available future options are laid out:

> Thus says the Lord: Go down to the house of the king of Judah, and speak there this word, and say: Hear the word of the Lord, O King of Judah, sitting on the throne of David—you, and your servants, and your people who enter these gates. Thus says the Lord: Act with justice and righteousness, and deliver from the hand of the oppressor anyone who has been robbed. And do no wrong or violence to the alien, the orphan, and the widow, or shed innocent blood in this place. For if you will indeed obey this word, then through the gates of this house shall enter kings who sit on the throne of David, riding in chariots and on horses, they, and their servants, and their people. But if you will not heed these words, I swear by myself, says the Lord, that this house shall become a desolation.

This text claims that, in this situation, two specific future possibilities are open to king and people, depending upon their exercise of justice. If they do justice, their future will take a certain form; if they do not do justice, their future will take a different shape. What people do and say regarding justice (and other matters) can—indeed will—have a genuine effect on the shape that their future, and the shape that others' future, will take. We must emphasize this point with people we encounter: what they do and say counts and will give shape to several possible futures.

So, finally, there *will be* a new heaven and a new earth; God *will* raise people from the dead. But between now and that future, what people do will make a difference, and it will make a difference to God and to the nature of the future of their own world.

To illustrate, one might suggest that God's creating of the new heaven and new earth is a quilt-making enterprise. Your patches and mine, which have been developed through our years of words and deeds, will contribute to the shape and color of that new quilt. What will those patches be like? How will those patches affect that future? What we do and say through the years will make a difference as to how our life and world will take shape.

As noted above, sometimes an unqualified language creeps into our talk about God and the shape of our future—that the future is "in God's hands" and settled. Perhaps, if we regularly qualified such a statement—such as, "the future is *ultimately* in God's hands"—we would be clearer and more convincing. But if we just say that the future is in God's hands, those who hear that claim could easily conclude that it makes little, if any, difference what they and we do about matters of, say, justice or the environment. Such a perspective regarding the future will turn off many a person to the word of the Bible about such matters, as well as to life in the church. Such a perspective could also lead, unfortunately, to a certain level of passivity relative to one's own life and health. A friend of mine had a close call in a car accident, and his response was: "It wasn't my time." As if there were a specific time determined by God for when each person would die! Smoke three packs of cigarettes a day; it doesn't matter—your time is all set. Take as many risks as you would like; no matter what you do, your time is set. But that's not *faith*; that's *fate*.

Prepare your own list: I will not get ready for my retirement; I will not take out insurance; I will not take care of my health. Or, more communally, I will not take care of the environment. I submit that all such behaviors are a violation of the biblical imperative: you shall not tempt the Lord your God. *Ultimately*, yes, we put ourselves in the hands of God, but between now and that future, we are called to get busy and help make a positive difference with regard to the potential shape of our future and the future of others.

There is a temporal succession, a before and after, in the divine life and relationship to life in the world. These types of texts make the most sense when one assumes that in creation God has chosen to relate to the world from within its structures of time. As has been noted, one might say that God is eternal but not timeless. God has freely chosen to enter into the time of the world in such a way that God truly shares in that history, and God thereby can be said to have a past, a present, and a future.[1]

One must speak of the *story* of God in some sense of that term. God genuinely chooses to get caught up in the relational and temporal journey of God's people and world. At the same time, unlike all creatures, God is eternal and is not subject to the ravages of time. The birth and death of Jesus are genuinely temporal events for God; in the fullness of time, God sent forth a Son (see Galatians 4:4). At the same time, what people do and say in the course of their life's journey makes a difference, not only for their own life and that of others; it makes a difference to the life of God. God and God's future are genuinely shaped by what creatures do and say.

The Future and Prophets

This temporal understanding of God gives us a somewhat different perspective on various biblical angles, including the work of the prophets. For example, one of the common definitions of "prophet"—namely, that the prophet is a predictor of the shape of the future—simply will not do. To use the language of prediction is to make the prophet's language about the future much more specific than that future actually is; generally, the prophets were not concerned about speaking with precision regarding future times and places. This perspective is evident in the fact that calendrical concerns are rare indeed in the biblical material, and in the comparatively rare examples of which we might speak, the prophet is either flat-out wrong (Jonah 3) or the number of years turned out to be inexact (Jeremiah 25).

Rather than constructing a specific timetable, the prophets almost always speak more generally of the future ("in that day" or "in the latter days" or "the days are surely coming"). The prophets do have a basic future orientation; there is little doubt about that. But it would be much truer to the prophetic message to speak of the prophet as one who proclaims or announces a word, often about the future. Several principles need to guide our thinking about the prophets and their word about the future.

First, there is seldom a literal correspondence between a prophecy and a fulfillment. By way of illustration: A father promises his young son in the early 1900s that, if he maintains certain patterns of behavior, the father will give him a horse and buggy on his twenty-first birthday. The years go by, and the son makes good on his end of the bargain; the time for fulfillment of the promise is at hand. But in the meantime Henry Ford has been at work, and Model Ts are on the streets. The last thing the son wants from his father is a horse and buggy. The father could say, "I made you a promise, and I am going to fulfill that promise precisely as I made it." But the son would

> It would be much truer to the prophetic message to speak of the prophet as one who proclaims or announces a word, often about the future.

rather the father change the form of the fulfillment of the promise and give him a Model T. Indeed, in order to be true to the promise, the form of the fulfillment would have to be changed.

So, the prophet's message is adapted to the time and place of the audience to which it is directed. By the time we get to Jesus, many of his contemporaries are looking for a literal fulfillment of some of these prophecies, something like God coming into their lives on a white horse and delivering them from the Romans. The disciples get past the literal form of God's promises and see that Jesus is indeed the one God has promised but in a form and content much more marvelous than what the prophets had ever imagined. Today, as well, various folks, in thinking about the future, are looking for a horse and buggy. And they may miss the car!

Second, there is often—though not always—a contingent element with respect to prophetic words of indictment and judgment. That is, the way in which people responded to the prophet could affect the fulfillment of a specific prophetic word, though all such contingencies were understood from within God's larger saving will for Israel and the world. Again, I offer an illustration: In some ways, God is like parents who play chess with young children, knowing that they could finally win the game if they chose. But because the parents value the relationship, they choose to play in a way that does not overpower the child. And, given this kind of relationship, as the children improve in their chess-playing abilities, the parents will have to cope with the increasingly sophisticated moves the children make. So the way in which the game will progress and finally be won, and the amount of time it will take, will change in light of the various moves the child makes. The shape of the future is determined not only by God but also by those to whom God speaks and by the nature of their lives.

For example, the Jeremiah 22:1–5 text discussed above speaks of two possible futures for Israel, depending on how they treat the disadvantaged among them. The people of God, indeed the larger creation of which they are a part, through the powers they have been given are capable of shaping the future in various ways—indeed, *giving shape to the future of God.* Two possible futures for God are laid out in these verses (and many others), and human actions are a significant factor in the nature of that future for God. The future is not simply in God's hands; divine decisions and actions are not the only things that will shape it.

What creatures do and say counts for the nature of that future as well.

The decisions that the people of God make in their lives and with regard to the lives of others matter to God because of the genuine relationship God has established with them—one in which the words and deeds of both parties to the relationship count. God knows that that is the case, so God takes into account what people say and do in moving into the future. Think of God as a seamstress or a weaver or a quilt-maker. God is one who takes the threads and the patches of our words and deeds and sews them into the quilt of our future, finally the future of God's new heaven and new earth. At the same time, we can be assured that God will see to it that nothing of value is lost in that future.

> God is one who takes the threads and the patches of our words and deeds and sews them into the quilt of our future, finally the future of God's new heaven and new earth.

There are people who think the earth is in its last minutes of existence; that God is about to wrap up the history of the world in our lifetime, and some people have been "clued in" regarding the details of its final stages (be assured, most of us are not among them!). These people think, given this short time frame, that we don't need to take any special care for the less fortunate; heaven will be theirs soon, anyway! And we don't need to take any special care for the environment: it's all going to be destroyed soon anyway! Such a "theology of demolition" is one of the more powerful forces inhibiting our practice of justice and our environmental considerations. We successfully passed the year 2000, but the Left Behind book series and other schemes are still selling like hotcakes; we will continue to be subjected to speculation about the details relative to the end of the world, as we have been for centuries.

One effect has been and will be that people get so caught up in thinking about the next world that their sense of responsibility for this world is diminished. As a layperson once told me: "Ever since I discovered this scenario about the end of the world, I quit making my weekly visits to the senior citizens' home and now spend that time reading my Bible and praying." In other words, how we think and speak and act about the imagined shape of the future can have a massive effect on how we think about those less fortunate than ourselves, and on our practice of justice more generally.

The Future and Moral Order

An integral part of the future of which the prophets often spoke had to do with judgment, and often the experience of violent judgment. For the prophets, the people would typically have to go through a time of judgment before the promise of salvation could be realized. In moving toward such a future, God acts in and through agents, both human and nonhuman. I recall some earlier reflections to clarify this point.

The created moral order is such an agent. That moral order might be defined as a complex, loose causal weave of act and consequence that God created. Creaturely actions, good and bad, will have consequences for that order and its future. That human sins have consequences, including violence, is ongoing testimony to the *proper* functioning of the moral order; this reality can be named the judgment of God. Just how God relates to the movement from sin to consequence in specific ways is difficult to sort out, not least because the Old Testament does not speak with one voice about the matter. But generally speaking, the relationship between sin and consequence is conceived in intrinsic ways rather than forensic terms; that is, consequences grow out of the deed itself rather than being imposed from without by God as a penalty or punishment. As an example of God's involvement regarding issues of judgment, see Ezekiel 22:31. God declares, "I have consumed them with the fire of my wrath." What that divine judgment entails is immediately stated: "I have returned [*natan*] their conduct upon their own heads."[2] Notably, God does not (need to) introduce judgment into the situation. God's creation works in such a way that human sins have effects; the destructive effects of human actions are already springing forth from the human deeds.

While this understanding could be expressed in language such as "your sins will find you out" or "you reap what you sow" (Proverbs 22:8; Galatians 6:7), Israel often—though not always (e.g., Hosea 4:1–3)—explicitly links God to the connection between sin and consequence. Interpreters have used several different formulations to speak of how God is involved: God midwifes, facilitates, sees to, puts in force, mediates, and completes the connection between sin and its effects. The same Hebrew word is used for the wicked deed and for the consequence of that deed, commonly translated "disaster" (*ra`ah* leads to *ra`ah;* *`awon* leads to *`awon*). The judgment experienced flows out of the people's own wickedness, which means that the God-created moral order is functioning appropriately.[3] Or, in the words of Romans 1:24, 26, 28, God gives people over to the consequences of their own choices.

The moral order, however, does not function in any mechanistic, precise, or inevitable way; that order is not a tight causal weave. The moral order is a loose weave. (To use a cloth image, it is more like burlap than silk.) Hence, Jeremiah can lament to God with these questions about the causal weave (Jeremiah 12:1): Why do all the treacherous thrive? Why are those people down the block who never go to church so wealthy? And so, it may be that the wicked will prosper, at least for a time, and the innocent will suffer (think about Job and the effects of natural evil he suffers) or get caught up in the effects of the sins of others (think of Israel in Egypt). What's more, as Ecclesiastes 9:11 states, "time and chance happen to them all"; in other words, there is an element of randomness in relating human deeds to suffering effects. One might even think of the randomness of the gene pool ("There is no lifeguard at the gene pool!").

One cannot, therefore, conclude that *all* experiences of suffering or violence are due to the actions of any individual or community. This is especially the case when considering *communal* violence. Innocents (children, for example) may suffer deeply in view of the interconnectedness of the world (about which Abraham complains mightily—Genesis 15:2–3). In the wake of the flood story, God promises not to do such an act ever again (see Genesis 9). In making such a promise, God freely chooses to be subject to this just order and not to interrupt it or otherwise interfere with its natural functioning. The nature of the divine involvement in such events cannot be factored out, except to say that the looseness of the causal weave does allow God to be at work in some unknown ways *within* "the system" without violating it or suspending the way in which the world works.

In the functioning of this moral order, God is a genuine agent. But God always, *always* works in and through non-divine agents. People's sins generate snowballing effects; God is active in the interplay of these sinful actions and their effects; "third parties" (e.g., Babylon) are used by God as agents for that judgment.[4] We learn from the prophets especially that both God and God's agents (e.g., Babylon under Nebuchadnezzar) are often the subject of the same destructive verbs.[5] In Jeremiah 13:14, for example, God speaks these words: "I will dash them one against another, parents and children together, says the Lord. I will not pity or spare or have compassion when I destroy them." In Jeremiah 21:7, however, "[*Nebuchadnezzar*] shall strike them down with the edge of the sword; he shall not pity them, or spare them, or have compassion." Again and again, the portrayal of God in the text is *conformed to the life of the agents God uses.* God is thereby associated in this world with a great

> God is a genuine agent. But God always, *always* works in and through non-divine agents.

deal of violence. A modern parallel might be cited, whereby God's work in the church is often associated with the work of agents like ourselves, and God's reputation suffers because God is thereby associated with an awful lot of, well, crap.

One might use the illustration of World War II, wherein God used allied armies to overcome Hitlerian hordes. But the agents often exceeded the divine mandate, as, for example, in the saturation bombing of Dresden and other cities. As noted above, God is not the only agent at work in such situations, ancient or modern, as if God could at any time push a button and "fix" matters. God is not a magician. Given God's determination to use such agents in working in the world, God's way into the future cannot be reduced to a simple divine decision to act. The agents in and through which God works can have an impact on the shape of that future that is sharply negative. Because of God's committed relationship to the world, no resolution will be simple, not even for God.

A remarkable number of prophetic texts speak of divine judgment on those nations that have been agents of God, such as Assyria and Babylonia (Jeremiah 25:12–14; 27:6–7; 50:1–51:64; Isaiah 10:12–19; 47:1–15; Zechariah 1:15). Their excessiveness at the expense of Israel made the land an "everlasting waste" (Jeremiah 25:12). The exercise of divine wrath against these nations demonstrates that they were not puppets in God's hand. These agents retained the power to make decisions and execute policies that flew in the face of the will of God in a given situation; the God active in these events is not irresistible. God risks what the agents will do with the mandate they have been given.

One element of that risk is, to say it again, that God's name will become associated with their excessive violence. This is, in fact, what has happened over the course of history, and it has complicated much reflection regarding the nature of the God of the Old Testament.

Another text (Jeremiah 42:10) reveals a divine regret regarding the violence experienced by Israel in the fall of Jerusalem: "I am sorry for the disaster that I brought upon you." God's response to Israel's suffering at the hands of overreaching agents is remarkable: "I am sorry." How are we to understand this striking divine admission? I think it is not a divine apology but carries the sense of genuine regret. The judgment and its painful effects proved to be more severe than God had intended, or perhaps even thought they would be. Hence, an evaluation of the work of God's own agents may take this form: They overdid it! They blew it! This interpretation seems especially apt in view of the excessiveness of Babylon in its many conquests.

Yet, God does not remove the divine self from responsibility for the use of means that resulted in an imperfect execution of the mandate. The genuineness of the relationship entails a divine constraint and restraint in the exercise of power in relation to these agents. God does not micromanage their activity, intervening to make sure every little thing is done correctly according to the divine will. Still, God, who does not foreknow absolutely what and how the agents will speak and act, accepts some responsibility for what has happened. "I'm sorry!" A remarkable divine exclamation! This text reveals something of the inner life of God, who uses agents that cannot be micromanaged and is deeply pained at the results (see, e.g., Jeremiah 8:18–9:19).[6]

God, however, is not bereft of resources to act in the midst of suffering. Indeed, suffering becomes a vehicle for divine action. God does not relate to suffering as a mechanic does to a car, seeking to "fix it" from the outside. God enters deeply into the suffering human situation and works for the necessary healing *from within*. For God to so enter into the suffering situation means that mourning will not be the last word.

> God enters deeply into the suffering human situation and works for the necessary healing *from within*.

These texts are testimony to a divine sovereignty that gives power over to the created for the sake of a relationship of integrity. At the same time, as discussed above, this way of relating to people—not least the use of agents prone to violence—reveals a divine vulnerability. In such a move, God opens up the divine self to the experience of hurt should things not go according to the divine will. And the actions of the agents often do go violently wrong, *despite* God's best efforts.

It may be said that God's most basic stance in the face of potential violence is nonviolence. See the divine offer in Jeremiah 38:17–18:

> Then Jeremiah said to Zedekiah, "Thus says the Lord, the God of hosts, the God of Israel, If you will only surrender to the officials of the king of Babylon, then your life shall be spared, and this city shall not be burned with

fire, and you and your house shall live. But if you do not surrender to the officials of the king of Babylon, then this city shall be handed over to the Chaldeans, and they shall burn it with fire, and you yourself shall not escape from their hand."

God makes clear that God does not want the destruction of Jerusalem. But in order to accomplish God's work in the world, God may respond in and through potentially violent agents (*every such agent* of God is potentially violent in some way) for the express purpose that sin and evil not go unchecked in the life of the world. In our reflections about such texts, we must certainly not set them aside just because they offend us; we must learn to read the Bible *against* ourselves, to let its texts be in our face.

But must we not also ask, Is everything violent in the Bible that offends us considered offensive? One thinks of the biblical absence of a condemnation of patriarchy or slavery, or the divine command of the wholesale slaughter of cities. Might the Bible itself contain an internal evaluative process that could help us consider this issue? It is conceivable that the biblical center (Exodus 34:6–7) could get us there, but that may not always be the case.

Another way into this conversation is to note the extent to which key biblical characters raise questions about God and make challenges regarding God's (anticipated) actions. One thinks of Abraham's challenge to God in Genesis 18:25, "Shall not the Judge of all the earth do what is just?" Or God's actions in and through Moses in Exodus 32:7–14, in the wake of the sin of the golden calf: Moses engages God with respect to the announced destruction of Israel, citing the tradition of the ancestral promises. God is responsive to human challenge and moves away from decisions made (in the case of Moses) or potentially does so (in the case of Abraham). These kinds of narrative testimonies invite Bible readers to engage in similar challenges to formulations regarding divine violence. This direction of thought is no simple task; it is a major issue needing sustained dialogue. And, disappointingly, no satisfactory explanation of this linkage of God and violence seems finally to

> **Because God suffers violence and the effects of violence, God thereby takes the violence into the divine self and makes possible a nonviolent future for the world.**

be possible. But some directions of thought are more fruitful in response than are others.

That God would stoop to become involved in such human cruelties as war and other forms of violence is finally not a matter for despair, but for hope. God does not simply give people up to experience violence. Again and again, God takes the side of those entrapped in violence and its effects and does so in such a way that God, entering deeply into the violent life of the world, personally bears that violence in order to bring about good purposes. The tears of the people are fully recognized by God; their desperate situation is named for what it really is. By choosing to participate in our messy stories, God's own self takes the road of suffering and death. Because God suffers violence and the effects of violence, God thereby takes the violence into the divine self and makes possible a nonviolent future for the world.

Where Are We?

We can helpfully use the image that human history is like a river, and all of us are in a raft on that river. For the prophets, the raft has often gotten to that point in the river right above a waterfall where the water behind a rocky lip sometimes eddies and is very calm and quiet, and the people are having such a fun time on the boat that they cannot hear the crashing of the falls. My question to readers is this: At what place in that river is the world of today? It is not too many years ago that people commonly thought that, with the fall of communism and some peace breakthroughs here and there, we were living in a less precarious world. We know today that that is not the case.

The prophets might ask the question of us, as they did of folks in their own time, What might current global crises have to say about ways we have treated our neighbors, not least the less fortunate among us? What might an economic crisis say about the way in which we have misused our wealth? A volume by Dan Via suggests, for example, that the experience of 9/11 should at least be considered a judgment of God against this nation for our practices of injustice.[7] Given the increasing gap between the more fortunate and the less fortunate among us, and our deep mistreatment and neglect of the needy, including millions of children living in poverty and without adequate health care, it seems to me that these experiences could be interpreted as signs that things are going to get worse, not better.

Again, where are we in the river? Is it possible that we are in that quiet water above the falls? Are we already being sucked into the pull of the falls and heading for an inevitable and terrifying trip over the brink? Is it already too late? I certainly think we need to work on behalf of the less fortunate as if it were not too late. And so, the word of the prophets to us may well be this: Repent, and let that repentance manifest itself in the shape of our life—that is, an especially concerted individual and corporate effort on behalf of the less fortunate among us. It may be that a future trip over the falls is inevitable. In that case, our only hope is in God, for life on the other side of disaster; the only future we can certainly anticipate is that God will pick us up from the rocks below the falls and send us on our way down the river once again.

Who will speak for God today regarding the deep and pervading crises relating to the poor and the needy in our society? We may not have much longer before God's patience with us has been exhausted and we experience not the end of *the* world but the end of *our* world.

Who will speak for God? It is important to stress that the word to be spoken by the prophets was shaped at least in part by their discernment of the word that the people most needed to hear, and/or by the nature of the critical moment. Prior to the fall of Samaria and Jerusalem, the prophets' words were mostly indictments for sin and announcements of judgment. One can see this in a prophet such as Amos (eighth century BCE), whose ministry was followed within a generation by a devastating disaster for his entire society as Israel fell to the Assyrian armies in 722 BCE. In other times and places, however, the prophet had a word of comfort to bring. After the fall of Jerusalem in 587 BCE, when the people of God were suffering in exile, the prophetic words were often much different—for example, Isaiah 40:1–2, "Comfort, O comfort my people, says your God. Speak tenderly to Jerusalem"—though these kinds of words are much less common in the prophets. A key task of the prophet, therefore, is discernment—that is, to seek to discern the nature of the crisis faced by the people in order to know what kind of word from God, or at least what emphases, to bring to bear on the moment. At the bedside of a dying Christian, you don't read the book of Amos; but perhaps in our own time and place, many individuals and congregations do need to hear Amos or prophets like him. Does this need for challenge include each of us at one time or another?

Jesus's own ministry was shaped by these texts from the law and the prophets. We tend to connect Jesus with only the promises of the prophets, that Jesus was the Messiah of whom the prophets spoke (though "Messiah" is not a word that the prophets ever use for the one who is to come). We need to remember that Jesus's ministry was decisively shaped by his reading of Old Testament texts concerning the less fortunate. The Gospel of Luke in particular has Jesus forming his entire ministry in these terms; see Luke 4:18–19, which quotes from Isaiah 61:1–2:

> The Spirit of the Lord is upon me, because he has anointed me to bring good news to the poor. He has

> sent me to proclaim release to the captives and recovery
> of sight to the blind, to let the oppressed go free, to pro-
> claim the year of the Lord's favor.

The "year of the Lord's favor" to which Jesus refers was the jubilee year, a twice-a-century, twelve-month period when the inequalities that had built up in the community over the previous fifty years could be rectified. Specifically, it was a time when everyone was released from all family debt and personal enslavement.

This redistribution of wealth and property is not based on a trickle-down theory of economic justice; it promises a waterfall. Not a hand-out, but a hand up. Not support for the needy in continuing poverty, but a genuine chance for a new beginning— back on the family farm and free of debt. It is noteworthy that these family values Jesus articulates are not expressed in explicitly moral terms, but in socioeconomic terms—namely, economic independence for every family and the personal and social dignity that goes with it. That Jesus was concerned about such economic realities can also be seen in his cleansing of the temple. And of course, during Jesus's ministry he was constantly reaching out to the less fortunate and the marginalized in his society: the poor, the outcast lepers, women, prostitutes, the demon-possessed, tax-collectors—name the outcast and Jesus touched their lives. Jesus's ministry announces that ministry must not be defined in simply spiritual terms, for Jesus is concerned about salvation in a full-bodied sense.

God has taken the initiative, freely entered into relationships with each of us, and empowered us for service. But having done so, God has decisively committed the divine self to be in a *genuine relationship* with us; God chooses to bind the divine self to that relationship and be committed to it. The Incarnation stands on this relational trajectory as the supreme exemplification of this divine relatedness and its irrevocability for God.

So, who will speak and act for God in such a time as this? Each of God's followers has the responsibility to pick up on this conversation and articulate a clear response in word and deed, thereby being true to our relationship with God.

God has taken the initiative, freely entered into relationships with each of us, and empowered us for service.

NOTES

CHAPTER 1: WHAT WE MEAN BY "RELATIONSHIP"

1. The difficult and ambiguous language of "control" with God as subject is more common than one might think. For recent reflections on this topic, see Thomas Oord, *The Uncontrolling Love of God: An Open and Relational Account of Providence* (Downers Grove, IL: IVP Academic, 2015).
2. Abraham Heschel, *The Prophets* (New York: Harper & Row, 1962), 486.
3. See Terence E. Fretheim, *The Suffering of God: An Old Testament Perspective,* OTL (Philadelphia: Fortress, 1984), 71.
4. Elizabeth Johnson, *She Who Is: The Mystery of God in Feminist Theological Discourse* (New York: Crossroad, 1992), 15.

CHAPTER 2: WHAT KIND OF GOD?

1. See William Loader's use of this phrase in, for example, "First Thoughts on Year B Gospel Passages from the Lectionary," http://wwwstaff.murdoch.edu.au/~loader/MkPentecost21.html.
2. Brian Wren, "God Talk and Congregational Song," *Christian Century,* May 3, 2000, 506.
3. Eberhard Jungel, *God as the Mystery of the World*, trans. Darrell Guder (Grand Rapids: Eerdmans, 1983), 330.
4. Walter Eichrodt, *Theology of the Old Testament,* vol. 1 (Philadelphia: Westminster, 1967).

CHAPTER 3: A RELATIONAL GOD

1. I develop these ideas further in my book *What Kind of God? Collected Essays of Terence E. Fretheim,* Michael J. Chan and Brent A. Strawn, eds. (Winona Lake, IN: Eisenbrauns, 2015).
2. See Terence E. Fretheim, "Christology and the Old Testament," in *Who Do You Say That I Am? Essays on Christology,* M. A. Powell and D. Bauer, eds. (Louisville: Westminster, 2000), 201–15. For example, early Christian reflections about God that led to Trinitarian thought were grounded not only in New Testament claims about Jesus and the Spirit.
3. See Joel Burnett, *Where Is God? Divine Absence in the Hebrew Bible* (Minneapolis: Fortress, 2010), for a different perspective on issues of divine absence.
4. For details on the two possible futures for God, see Terence E. Fretheim, *Jeremiah,* Smyth and Helwys Bible Commentary (Macon, GA: Smith & Helwys, 2002), 328–29.

CHAPTER 4: AN EVERLASTING FAITHFULNESS

1. See Walter Brueggemann, *A Commentary on Jeremiah: Exile and Homecoming* (Grand Rapids: Eerdmans, 1998), 121, 142, 152, 278.

CHAPTER 5: FULL-BODIED SALVATION

1. Mark Powell, "Salvation in Luke-Acts," *Word and World* 12 (1992), 5.
2. See Patrick Miller, *Interpreting the Psalms* (Minneapolis: Fortress, 1986), 110.

CHAPTER 7: CHANGE AND SUFFERING

1. See other texts regarding divine suffering in Terence E. Fretheim, *The Suffering of God: An Old Testament Perspective*, OTL (Philadelphia: Fortress, 1984), especially 106–48.

2. Terence E. Fretheim, "Suffering God and Sovereign God in Exodus: A Collision of Images," *Horizons in Biblical Theology* 11, no. 1 (January 1, 1989): 37–38.
3. For detail, see Fretheim, *The Suffering of God*, 107–48.
4. See Joseph Jensen, "Immanuel," ABD, III, 392–95.
5. See Terence E. Fretheim, *Creation Untamed: The Bible, God, and Natural Disasters* (Baker: Grand Rapids, 2010), 3–4.

CHAPTER 9: FOR THE GOOD OF ALL

1. For a treatment of divine wrath, see Terence E. Fretheim, "Theological Reflections on the Wrath of God in the Old Testament," *Horizons in Biblical Theology* 24 (2002), 1–26.
2. See Terence E. Fretheim, *The Suffering of God: An Old Testament Perspective,* OTL (Philadelphia: Fortress, 1984), 45–59.
3. See Terence E. Fretheim, *Exodus,* Interpretation (Louisville: John Knox, 1991), 106.
4. For detail, see Fretheim, *The Suffering of God*, 60–78.
5. See Fretheim, *The Suffering of God*, 66–67.

CHAPTER 10: AN ELEMENT OF UNCERTAINTY

1. See Terence E. Fretheim, *The Suffering of God: An Old Testament Perspective,* OTL (Philadelphia: Fortress, 1984), especially 66–67.

CHAPTER 11: THE GIFT OF PRAYER

1. See Terence E. Fretheim, "Prayer in the Old Testament: Creating Space in the World for God," in *A Primer on Prayer*, ed. Paul R. Sponheim (Philadelphia: Fortress, 1988), 54.

CHAPTER 12: SHARING POWER

1. See Terence E. Fretheim, *The Suffering of God: An Old Testament Perspective*, OTL (Philadelphia: Fortress, 1984); Thomas J. Oord,

The Uncontrolling Love of God: An Open and Relational Account of Providence (Downers Grove, IL: IVP Academic, 2015).

2. Lewis B. Smedes, "What's God Up To? A Father Grieves the Loss of a Child," *Christian Century* 120, no. 9 (2003), 39.

3. The phrase "all flesh" includes animals (Genesis 6:19; 7:15–16, 8:17), not least in view of 9:5, where animals are held accountable for taking the life of another; this may be a reference to carnivores, the eating of blood, as a violation of a vegetarian way of life.

4. It could be claimed that floods per se are *not* the effect of human violence; such natural events are an integral part of the world that God created. Rather, it is the range and intensity of the flood that is understood to grow out of human violence.

5. Sometimes God as subject stands in a prominent position (e.g., Jeremiah 19:7–9); in other texts, God's stance is more passive (e.g., Hosea 4:1–3), even withdrawing (Isaiah 64:6–7).

6. God's relationship to Babylon changes in view of its conduct as the agent of judgment. By its excessively destructive behaviors Babylon opens itself up to reaping what it has sown (Jeremiah 50:29; 51:24). God turns against God's own agent on the basis of justice (even Israel: see Exodus 22:21–24). Such texts (cf. the Oracles against the Nations, Jeremiah 46–51) assume that moral standards are known by the nations, which are held accountable to them.

7. The translation of *niham* is difficult (NRSV, "be sorry"; NAB, "regret"; NIV/NEB, "grieve"). Each of these translations carries the sense of a pained divine response to God's own actions. See the discussion of William McKane, *A Critical and Exegetical Commentary on Jeremiah*, vol. 2 (Edinburgh: T&T Clark, 1986), 1033. For an earlier treatment of this pericope and other related texts, see Terence E. Fretheim, "'I Was Only a Little Angry': Divine Violence in the Prophets," *Interpretation* 58, no. 4 (2004): 365–75.

8. One thinks of the difference between, say, "mind control" and "crowd control." See Oord, *The Uncontrolling Love of God*.

CHAPTER 13: BOTH SETTLED AND UNSETTLED

1. For more detail on divine temporality, see Terence E. Fretheim, "Jeremiah's God Has a Past, a Present, and a Future," in *The Book of Jeremiah: Composition, Reception, and Interpretation*, eds. Jack R. Lundbom, Bradford A. Anderson, Craig A. Evans (Leiden: Brill, 2018), 455–75.

2. I have found over fifty Old Testament texts that link divine wrath with such formulations (e.g., Psalm 7:12–16; Isaiah 59:17–18; 64:5–9; Jeremiah 6:11, 19; 7:18–20; 21:12–14; 44:7–8; 50:24–25; Lamentations 3:64–66).

3. The understanding of *ra`ah* issuing in *ra`ah* may be observed in several formulations. God brings disaster (*ra`ah*), which is "the fruit of *their* schemes" (Jeremiah 6:19). Or, "I will pour out *their* wickedness upon them" (Jeremiah 14:16). Or, God gives to all "according to *their* ways, according to the fruit of *their* doings" (Jeremiah 17:10). Ezekiel 7:27 puts the matter in these terms: "According to their own judgments I will judge them." Like fruit, the consequence grows out of the deed itself. God's activity is "built into" the order of creation, the way in which the world works.

4. See Terence E. Fretheim, *The Suffering of God; An Old Testament Perspective*, OTL (Philadelphia: Fortress, 1984), 77. This dynamic understanding of sin and its effects can also be observed in the use of the verb *paqad*, "visit." Its translation as "punish" in NRSV is often problematic, as in Jeremiah 21:14: "I will punish you according to the fruit of your doings." A more literal translation is more accurate: "I will visit upon you the fruit of your doings" (see also Jeremiah 5:9; 14:10). We need to consider whether the word "punish" is ever an appropriate translation of the verb *paqad* (see the related noun *pequdah*, often translated "punishment"—e.g., Jeremiah 46:21). See the formulation of Gerhard von Rad regarding Israel's "synthetic view of life" and Israel's lack of punishment language in his *Old Testament Theology*, vol. 1, trans. D. M. G. Stalker (New York: Harper & Row, 1964), 265. The practical implications

of the translation of *paqad* can be seen in a comparison of RSV and NRSV in Exodus 20:5b. RSV translates "visiting the iniquity of the fathers upon the children"; NRSV, however, changes that to read, "punishing children for the iniquity of parents." Strangely, the NRSV translates the same formulation in Exodus 34:7 as "visiting the iniquity of the fathers upon the children."

5. For an extensive list, see Terence E. Fretheim, *Jeremiah*, Smyth and Helwys Bible Commentary (Macon, GA: Smyth & Helwys, 2002), 36.
6. For a discussion of divine suffering, see especially Fretheim, *The Suffering of God*, 107–48.
7. Dan Via, *Divine Justice, Divine Judgment: Rethinking the Judgment of Nations* (Minneapolis: Fortress, 2007).

THEOLOGY FOR CHRISTIAN MINISTRY

Informing and inspiring Christian leaders and communities to proclaim God's *Word* to a *World* God created and loves. Articulating the fullness of both realities and the creative intersection between them.

Word & World Books is a partnership between Luther Seminary, the board of the periodical *Word & World*, and Fortress Press.

Books in the series include:

Future Faith: Ten Challenges Reshaping Christianity in the 21st Century by Wesley Granberg Michaelson (2018)

Liberating Youth from Adolescence by Jeremy P. Myers (2018)

Elders Rising: The Promise and Peril of Aging by Roland Martinson (2018)

I Can Do No Other: The Church's New Here We Stand Moment by Anna M. Madsen (2019)

Intercultural Church: A Biblical Vision for an Age of Migration by Safwat Marzouk (2019)

Rooted and Renewing: Imagining the Church's Future in Light of Its New Testament Origins by Troy M. Troftgruben (2019)

Journeying in the Wilderness: Forming Faith in the 21st Century by Terri Martinson Elton (2020)

God So Enters into Relationships That . . .: A Biblical View by Terence E. Fretheim (2020)